DIS

music
of the
Romantic Era

by

David McCleery

Published by Naxos Books, an imprint of Naxos Rights International Ltd
© Naxos Books 2007
www.naxosbooks.com

Printed and bound in China by Leo Paper Group
Design and layout: Hannah Davies, Fruition – Creative Concepts
Music compiled by David McCleery
Editor: Genevieve Helsby
Map illustrator: Arthur Ka Wai Jenkins
Timeline: Hugh Griffith
All photographs © AKG Images

A CIP Record for this book is available from the British Library.

ISBN: 978-1-84379-236-9

Contents

Website

Log onto **www.naxos.com/naxosbooks/discoverromantic** and hear over two hours of music, all referred to in the text.

To access the website you will need:

ISBN: 9781843792369
Password: Gretchen

website Streamed at 64Kbps to provide good-quality sound
website Easy links to view and purchase any of the original CDs from which the extracts are taken.

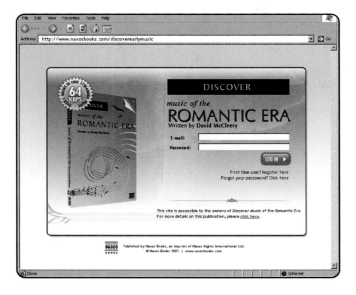

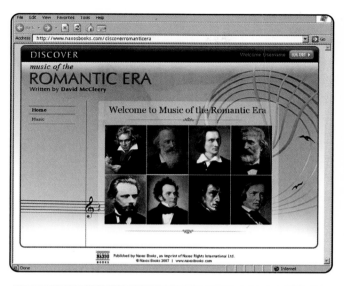

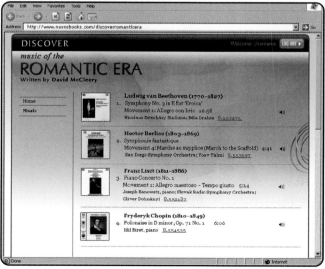

music
of the
Romantic Era

by

David McCleery

The Cross in the Mountains, *c. 1812,*
by *Caspar David Friedrich (1774–1840)*

I. The Dawn of the Romantic Era

What Was the Romantic Era?

The nineteenth century was a time of great political, cultural and artistic upheaval in the western world. The dream of an ideal society spread throughout the consciousness of Europe and the New World, and it was a dream that people were determined to turn into a reality. Not only were they inspired by 'liberté, égalité et fraternité' (the motto of post-revolutionary France), they sought to return to a natural state of being, one in which the individual would seek truth in his own heart and not in the political and religious conventions of the day. But for this perfect world to be achieved, both politically and personally, things would have to get worse before they got better; and aside from this prevailing spirit of hope and optimism, the era now dubbed the 'Romantic' period was dogged by wars, poverty and disease. None of these would feature in today's interpretation of the word 'romantic', so how did the term come about?

The word itself derives from the Old French word 'romanz' and refers to the many stories of heroism, chivalry and passion – the romances – of medieval times. These were written in such languages as French, Spanish, Italian and

Portuguese – languages which grew out of Latin and therefore came to be termed the 'romance' languages. It is the extremes of emotion contained in these stories that led to our modern definition of the word 'romantic' and which are key qualities of Romantic music.

In the seventeenth and eighteenth centuries people lived in deference to either the Church or the State, and major advances in the fields of physics, astronomy, biology and medicine resulted in a belief that the world could be fully explained by science and reason. Society had a highly regulated and ordered quality, against which people eventually started to rebel. Artists began to look beyond the well-established strict rules of form in order to express themselves. In the late-eighteenth and nineteenth centuries painters, writers and musicians began to find inspiration in the art of medieval times, responding to the heightened emotion contained in the romances as well as the tragic songs of 'courtly love' performed by the troubadours in medieval France. The German Romantic writer Goethe wrote books in a medieval, Gothic vein and they proved hugely influential over the next hundred years. *Faust*, perhaps the most famous of all his works, tells the story of a man so hopelessly in love with a woman that he sells his soul to the Devil to have his love reciprocated, if only for a short time. This story was the subject of several operas and oratorios by Romantic composers, such as Gounod, Liszt and Berlioz. There was also a renewed surge of interest in the plays of Shakespeare, whose plots involving love, nature and magic appealed very much to the Romantic spirit.

Composers in particular, searching for ways to express this heightened emotion, delved deep into their inner selves and made musical discoveries which they experienced in almost religious terms. Beethoven believed that music was 'a higher revelation than all wisdom and philosophy' and Rossini claimed that music was 'a sublime art which moves the earthly passions with celestial harmony'. In exploring their own emotions, composers were developing a sense that they were a channel through which something divine was flowing. This belief in the importance of the individual was typical of society's fast-changing viewpoint. The common man had for too long toiled away for the glory of the State: it was now time to glorify his own rights and traditions. Thus there was a renewed interest in traditional peasant folk culture, which led to a strengthening of national identity throughout Europe.

A deep love of nature became very fashionable. Many young men who went on the Grand Tour (the eighteenth-century equivalent of a gap year) found that they were less interested in the measured and calculated splendour of the classical Italian cities they visited than in the mysterious, wild and unknowable beauty of the Alps which they traversed en route. As we shall see in later chapters, nature featured strongly as a source of inspiration in nineteenth-century music.

Aside from the elements mentioned above, Romantic composers, breaking away from the formal strictures of the preceding 'Classical' period, sought to develop the existing genres and invent new ones. Symphonies, concertos and operas grew in size and stature, as did the orchestras (and singers) that performed them. Yet the Romantic era was not just about everything becoming bigger. It was an age of extremes, and a tiny chamber work of quiet, aching intensity is just as characteristic of the period as an epic symphonic work. 'Programme music' (music that tells a story or paints a picture) was an important new genre and led to the development of the symphonic poem, which will be explored later. Often inspired by a composer's love of nature or of another person, programme music was the perfect vehicle for Romantic expression. Moreover, Romantic composers often sought to unify their works in a variety of different ways – sometimes by having the same theme or melody throughout the different movements of a symphony, or at other times by linking movements together so that a whole work is played without a break.

It is not possible to give a comprehensive and exhaustive list of qualities contained in music of the Romantic period: each composer's personal journey led to many contradictory trends and to many clashes of artistic opinion. Perhaps the defining quality is a break from the formal conventions of the eighteenth century. But when we come to explore the music, we can be sure to find passion and intense emotion, as well as an obsession with nature, folk traditions, nationalist fervour and many manifestations of the individual's self-expression.

The Rise of Romanticism

Artists have been regarded with suspicion throughout history. Back in the fourth century BC, Plato claimed that 'art is subversive to the State'. Even today, a similar attitude prevails: many people would regard the winning artworks of the UK's annual Turner Prize (named after one of the greatest Romantic painters) as unrepresentative of the high moral fibre of good and decent society. However, as the Romantic era dawned, and the individual became increasingly empowered, artists were at least able to do something about their social position. They had traditionally been thought of as merely craftsmen or artisans whose job it was to create art or music for the benefit of the Church or the State. By the end of the eighteenth century, they were beginning to see themselves as geniuses with a rare talent. When Haydn entered the service of Prince Esterházy as a court composer in the 1760s, his fame was primarily due to his association with the Prince; by the time of Haydn's death in 1809, the Esterházy court was famous due to its connection with the composer.

Haydn, however, was a Classical composer: the Romantic era of music began two or three decades later than that of literature and philosophy. A German writer called F.M. Klinger published a play in 1777 called *Sturm und Drang* ('Storm and Stress') after which an early Romantic artistic movement was named. This movement encompassed subjectivity, enthusiasm for nature, rebellion against accepted standards and a full rein to emotional expression. 'Sturm und Drang' was more influential on the literary than on the musical scene. Haydn did write a series of symphonies which later became known as the 'Sturm und Drang' symphonies but, despite the use of minor keys and the odd dramatic effect, these works really remain firmly within the eighteenth-century Classical tradition.

The writer and philosopher Jean-Jacques Rousseau (1712–1778) was one of the first key figures in Romantic thought. He opposed the rule of reason, believing in an order based not on intellect but on the truth of nature. Over the course of several decades the seat of European philosophical thought shifted from France to Germany, where many increasingly impenetrable books and treatises on philosophy were written that built on Rousseau's theories. Immanuel Kant (1724–1804) was one such writer. In his *Critique of Pure Reason* he argued that, contrary to the views of Sir Isaac Newton in the late seventeenth and early eighteenth centuries, scientific exploration only served to reveal how mysterious and unfathomable the world actually is. His core message, put extremely simply, was that you should act as you would like others to act. Such views shook the hierarchical establishment of eighteenth-century society, which, combined with a growing unease among the lower and middle classes, led eventually to civil unrest.

The American Revolution, which culminated in the Declaration of Independence from British rule in 1783 (see pages 16–17), proved that rebellion against the establishment could be successful. And nowhere did this message strike a stronger chord than in France, where the aristocratic classes were ruling the country like feudal lords, levying crippling taxes on an increasingly disenchanted and deprived peasant class. Emboldened by contemporary thought, which was embodied in the works of writers such as Rousseau, the middle classes revolted, and on 14 July 1789 the storming of the Bastille heralded the start of the French Revolution. However, change was not as everyone had expected. The King and Queen were deposed and eventually executed, and there followed the years of terror, during which large numbers met their destiny at the hands, or rather the blade, of Madame Guillotine.

New hope came with the appointment of a more moderate regime, and the young general Napoleon Bonaparte rose through the ranks of the army, determined to realise his Romantic ideals of uniting France and establishing both social and legal equality throughout the country. However, as his power increased so did his political ambition – and his ego. He invaded country after country, placing his friends and family in positions of political power, only to be stopped, first in Moscow in 1812 (a Russian victory commemorated seventy years later by Tchaikovsky in his *1812* overture), then at Leipzig by the Russians, Austrians and Prussians, and later at Waterloo by the British. He lived his last years in exile on the island of St Helena and died in 1821, leaving France with a legacy of further volatile decades.

Napoleon demonstrated how the rise of the individual – the Romantic ideal – could become misdirected and destructive. He was motivated by a worthy dream, and in many ways he did achieve much that was beneficial to the citizens of France; but his ruthless political ambition and ultimate failure left the French unsure about the benefits of pursuing the revolutionary values he stood for. This may go some way towards explaining why French music, with a few notable exceptions, was rather conservative for much of the nineteenth century and did not make a vast mark on musical history. In spite of this, it is difficult to overstate the wide-

From the Declaration of Independence

When in the Course of human events, it becomes necessary for one people to dissolve the political bands which have connected them with another, and to assume among the powers of the earth, the separate and equal station to which the Laws of Nature and of Nature's God entitle them, a decent respect to the opinions of mankind requires that they should declare the causes which impel them to the separation.

We hold these truths to be self-evident, that all men are created equal, that they are endowed by their Creator with certain unalienable Rights, that among these are Life, Liberty and the pursuit of Happiness. —That to secure these rights, Governments are instituted among Men, deriving their just powers from the consent of the governed, —That whenever any Form of Government becomes destructive of these ends, it is the Right of the People to alter or to abolish it, and to institute new Government, laying its foundation on such principles and organizing its powers in such

form, as to them shall seem most likely to effect their Safety and Happiness. Prudence, indeed, will dictate that Governments long established should not be changed for light and transient causes; and accordingly all experience hath shewn, that mankind are more disposed to suffer, while evils are sufferable, than to right themselves by abolishing the forms to which they are accustomed. But when a long train of abuses and usurpations, pursuing invariably the same Object evinces a design to reduce them under absolute Despotism, it is their right, it is their duty, to throw off such Government, and to provide new Guards for their future security. —Such has been the patient sufferance of these Colonies; and such is now the necessity which constrains them to alter their former Systems of Government. The history of the present King of Great Britain [George III] is a history of repeated injuries and usurpations, all having in direct object the establishment of an absolute Tyranny over these States.

ranging influence Napoleon had on the course of history: his example provided inspiration to revolutionaries all over the world, such as the great liberator Simón Bolívar (who freed much of South America from Spanish colonial rule) and arguably the greatest-ever musical revolutionary: Ludwig van Beethoven.

II. A Musical Revolution

Ludwig van Beethoven (1770–1827)

**"Keep your eyes on him; some day he will give
the world something to talk about"**

W.A. Mozart, speaking of Beethoven in 1787

Ludwig van Beethoven (1770–1827)

Beethoven was born in Bonn in 1770. His father was a second-rate court musician, and a temperamental alcoholic who was bitterly disappointed by the fact that his musical career would never rise above the level of mediocrity. He obsessively laid all his lost hopes of musical greatness onto Ludwig, forcing him to practise the piano at all hours of the day and night. This did not make growing up in the Beethoven household easy; but, as they say, every cloud has a silver lining, and possibly this harsh and sometimes frightening upbringing was responsible to some extent for the development of Beethoven's extraordinary drive, determination and perfectionism.

At the age of twenty-two Beethoven moved to Vienna, where he established himself as a pianist and composer. He took composition lessons from Haydn (from whom he later claimed to have learned nothing) and frequently entered the virtuoso piano competitions which were very popular at the time. He almost always won these, and the established Viennese virtuosi were astounded by the talents of this young unknown musician from a provincial backwater.

One of the most remarkable facts about Beethoven is his deafness. The devastating effect it had on him is made clear in a letter, written to his brothers in 1802 and now referred to as the Heiligenstadt Testament (named after the spa town where he was staying when he wrote it), which hints that it had led him to contemplate suicide (see pages 22–3). He first became aware of degenerative hearing problems in the late 1790s, and by 1816 he was profoundly deaf. How could a composer produce such ground-breaking music without the one sense that was most important to him? It could be that his enforced detachment from the world of sound encouraged his musical imagination to run wild, leading him to revolutionise the art form.

From the very start of his career, Beethoven had deliberately set out to expand the boundaries of the hitherto unchallenged musical conventions of the eighteenth century. His Piano Sonata, Op. 26 (1800–1) opens with an *Andante* theme and variations (instead of the standard brisk and energetic *Allegro*), something normally reserved for second movements. This may not seem outrageous today, but to contemporary audiences it would have seemed like the musical equivalent of serving the main course before the starter. In other early piano sonatas he wrote four movements instead of the usual three; his sonata structure therefore resembled that of a symphony. His first two symphonies (written in 1800 and 1802 respectively) sound conventional today, but when they were first performed critics attacked the heaviness of the orchestration, in which increased importance was given to the wind instruments.

However, those who had been surprised by the sound of the first two symphonies must have been open-mouthed as they listened to the Third. Beethoven originally dedicated his Third Symphony (website 1) (written in 1804) to Napoleon, who until then had been fighting tirelessly for the rights of the common man. But when Napoleon declared himself Emperor, Beethoven was so infuriated that he ripped out the title page containing the dedication and renamed the symphony 'Eroica' ('Heroic'), by which name it is known today. At over forty-five minutes long, the 'Eroica' was

Beethoven's Heiligenstadt Testament

Oh ye men, who consider me to be hostile, obstinate or misanthropic, how unjust you are to me, for you do not know the secret cause of that which makes me seem so to you. My heart and my soul, since my childhood, have ever been filled with tender feelings of good will: I was even ready to perform great deeds. But consider that for six years now I have been afflicted with an incurable condition, made worse by incompetent physicians, deceived for year after year by the hope of an improvement and now obliged to face the prospect of a permanent disability, the healing of which may take years or may even prove to be quite impossible. Born with an ardent, lively temperament, and also inclined to the distractions of society, I was, at an early age, obliged to seclude myself and to live my life in solitude. If, once in a while, I attempted to ignore all this, oh how harshly would I be driven back by the doubly sad experience of my bad hearing; yet it was not possible for me to say: speak louder, shout, for I am deaf. Alas, how would it be possible for me to admit to a weakness of the one sense that should be perfect to a higher degree in me than in others, the one sense which I once possessed in the highest perfection, a perfection that few others of my profession have ever possessed. No, I cannot do it. So forgive me if you see me draw back from your company which I would so gladly share. My misfortune is doubly

hard to bear, inasmuch as I will be misunderstood. For me there can be no recreation in the society of others, no intelligent conversation, no mutual exchange of ideas; only as much as is required by the most pressing needs can I venture into society. I am obliged to live like an outcast. If I venture into the company of men, I am overcome by a burning terror, inasmuch as I fear to find myself in the danger of allowing my condition to be noticed. What humiliation when someone standing next to me could hear from a distance the sound of a flute whereas I heard nothing. Or, someone could hear the shepherd singing, and that also I did not hear. Such experience brought me near to despair. It would have needed little for me to put an end to my life. It was art only that held me back. Ah, it seemed to me to be impossible to leave the world before I had brought forth all that I felt destined to bring forth. Almighty God, Thou lookest down into my innermost being; Thou knowest that the love of mankind and the desire to do good dwell therein. Oh men, when you once shall read this, reflect then that you have wronged me. You, my brothers, as soon as I am dead, if Professor Schmidt be still alive, request him in my name to describe my malady, and let him attach this written document to the report of my ailment, so that, as far as possible, the world may be reconciled with me after my death.

significantly longer than any previous symphony. The drive, energy and dramatic climaxes heard in the first movement were unprecedented in symphonic writing. In the middle of this movement there is a section lasting forty-five seconds (beginning at 7'58") in which the rhythm is thrown into such confusion that the listener loses all sense of where the beat lies. At 10'58" Beethoven plays a musical joke, giving the horn a false entry, as if the player has lost his way and come in too early. None of the techniques used in this symphony is absolutely new, but never before had they been used on such a scale. Other elements in the work, such as the emotional intensity of the second movement, broke the boundaries of symphonic writing and as such the 'Eroica' Symphony heralded the start of Romanticism in music. Two hundred years after the event it is difficult to understand how challenging this work was to a contemporary audience; but despite the fact that its premiere left even his most loyal supporters wondering if he had not gone one step too far, Beethoven never had any problems finding artistic patrons to fund his endeavours. Throughout his life, he regularly received generous amounts of money from such illustrious supporters as the Princes Lichnowsky, Kinsky and Lobkowitz, Archduke Rudolf and Count Andreas Razumovsky (to whom Beethoven dedicated three of his best-loved string quartets).

Beethoven continued to develop and innovate the symphony throughout his career. The famous opening motif of the Fifth, representing 'fate knocking', appears throughout the work, providing thematic unity between the movements. This was a new idea, and one which was to assume great importance over the course of the nineteenth century. The

Sixth Symphony (the 'Pastoral') was the first important example of programme music – music inspired by a non-musical idea. Each movement was given a programmatic title (e.g. 'the awakening of happy feelings upon arriving in the country'), mostly deriving from a typically Romantic appreciation of nature, and Beethoven's evocative score developed the symphony in yet another new direction.

In 1824 Beethoven wrote his final, Ninth, symphony which lasts over an hour and contains a triumphant choral setting of Schiller's *Ode to Joy* in the last movement. By this time he had established such a monumental prototype for the Romantic symphonic cycle that many composers spent years of their careers feeling too intimidated even to try to build upon it.

Beethoven's music was not merely about expansive scale and the grand gesture. He loved to demonstrate his breathtaking pianistic skills, but tended not to write ostentatious solo parts in his own concertos. Though often technically demanding for the soloist, Beethoven's concertos for piano (which form the bulk of his concerto output) are more like symphonic dialogues between soloist and orchestra, rather than the showy virtuoso solo pieces with orchestral accompaniment that typified the contemporary trend for concerto writing. Like the majority of his music, Beethoven's concertos concentrated more on an internalised mode of expression rather than a more frivolous, externalised one.

By 1816, as well as being profoundly deaf, Beethoven was suffering from chronic abdominal complaints. His behaviour became erratic, leading some to believe he had gone mad. His brother Caspar Carl had recently died, leaving a wife and son. For five years, Beethoven tried, ultimately unsuccessfully, to gain legal custody of his nephew Karl, as he felt (unfairly it would seem) that his sister-in-law was unfit to be a mother. This bitter and obsessive struggle was damaging to both uncle and nephew, and led to Karl making an unsuccessful suicide attempt. From this point Beethoven's health deteriorated steadily until he died in 1827, aged fifty-seven.

Beethoven was by all accounts a temperamental and difficult man; but those who knew him well also described his generous, kind and exuberant nature, which can be heard in so much of his music. He never married, tending to fall regularly for unavailable women, often members of the aristocracy. His deafness, abdominal complaints and turbulent relationship with his nephew and sister-in-law made his latter years deeply troubled. Yet the music of this period does not seem to betray any of these difficulties, being imbued instead with a heightened sense of spiritual awareness which is often difficult to fathom – especially in the case of his late string quartets. Beethoven undoubtedly was the composer who bridged the Classical and Romantic periods. The question of whether he should be thought of as a Romantic or primarily a transitional composer is a controversial one. However, considering the visionary and radical musical advances that he made, along with the great emotional power and depths of his music, there is a very strong argument to suggest that he was indeed a true Romantic.

III. A Radical New Musical Language

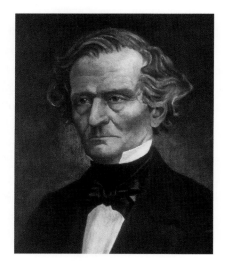

Hector Berlioz (1803–1869)

**"Love can give no idea of music; but music
can give an idea of love. Why separate them?
They are the two wings of the soul"**

Hector Berlioz, from his *Mémoires* (1870)

Beethoven's pioneering example broke open the floodgates of musical innovation. In the generation of composers that followed him, there were many who abandoned the traditions of the previous century. They invented new genres, and reworked existing ones such as the symphony into forms that would have been unrecognisable to audiences just twenty or thirty years before. Their music created extreme reactions, horrifying some but delighting others. Many of these composers were also virtuoso pianists: they wrote dazzling pieces which they themselves would play in concert, and their stunned audiences elevated them to the status of heroes. Thus the cult of the celebrity was born – a phenomenon with which we are all too familiar today. We will start by looking at a composer who in fact never learnt to play the piano, but whose ground-breaking music marked a dramatic departure from the musical conventions of the past.

Hector Berlioz (1803–1869)

Most French music from the nineteenth century tended to be fairly unadventurous in style. The most significant exception that proves this rule is the music of Hector Berlioz. He was born near Grenoble in 1803, and his father, a doctor, was very keen for the boy to follow in his footsteps. At the age of seventeen Berlioz moved to Paris to embark half-heartedly on his medical studies but he was soon offered a place at the Paris Conservatoire. His father reluctantly agreed to let him change direction, registering his disapproval by considerably reducing Berlioz's allowance.

Although French composers were not leading the way in new musical trends, Paris was a major European centre of opera and many of Berlioz's musical innovations derive from the operatic tradition. He also loved the theatre, and on 11 September 1827 he attended a performance of *Hamlet* which changed his life. The role of Ophelia was played by a young Irish actress called Harriet Smithson, with whom Berlioz immediately became obsessed. He spent much of the next two years attending her performances when he got the chance, writing her letters declaring his passion, and making desperate attempts to meet her, which she consistently thwarted. Today he might be labelled a stalker, but in the nineteenth century this was standard behaviour for a Romantic genius.

Berlioz's infatuation with Harriet Smithson led in 1830 to the composition of the wildly imaginative *Symphonie fantastique* (website 2). Subtitled 'An Episode in the Life of an Artist', it was probably the first ever autobiographical symphony to be written. In it, the object of the artist's desire (Harriet, though she is not mentioned by name in Berlioz's programme for the work) is represented by an *idée fixe*, or recurring theme, which appears in different guises throughout the piece. This technique had its origins in the 'reminiscence motif', which had been a common technique in opera since the late eighteenth century. The reminiscence motif was a tune assigned to a particular character and heard whenever that character appeared on stage.

In each of the five movements Berlioz provides a different scenario for his obsession. He daydreams about her in the first; in the second he catches a glimpse of her at a ball; in the third, thunder darkens an otherwise idyllic country scene when he realises that his love is unrequited. The fourth movement is entitled 'Marche au supplice' or 'March to the Scaffold': in a state of desperation and knowing that his love is hopeless, the artist has taken opium and dreams that he is being marched to the guillotine, having murdered his beloved. The movement is full of huge contrasts between louds and softs (e.g. at 0'59") which would have sounded extremely modern to contemporary audiences. You can hear the atmosphere of the march building to a frenzy as the music rises up and up at 2'52", and as the insistent driving rhythm is hammered out at 3'32". Suddenly, at 4'09", there is a brief reprieve as the artist's last thoughts are of his love, and we hear the *idée fixe* played ethereally on the clarinet. But his fate is sealed and, as he is beheaded, the *pizzicato* (plucked) strings depict the head falling into the bucket (4'18"), followed by the triumphal brass chords representing the jubilant crowd, delighted at their afternoon's entertainment. The final movement of the piece is set in hell where Berlioz depicts a witches' Sabbath, and this time the *idée fixe* is heard in a horribly distorted version.

One of Berlioz's greatest legacies was his highly imaginative use of orchestral instruments to colour his music, and in 1843 he published a treatise on orchestration which even today is regarded as one of the most important ever written. The *Symphonie fantastique* added harps, cor anglais and ophicleide (similar to the modern-day tuba) to the standard symphony orchestra; these were instruments which were normally heard only in opera orchestras.

After Harriet Smithson attended a performance of the *Symphonie fantastique* and realised that she was the subject of this astounding work, she agreed to meet Berlioz: the pair married in 1833. Harriet's career flagged and ultimately failed following an ankle injury. Her increasing jealousy of Berlioz's success put an unbearable strain on their relationship, and the couple separated ten years later. After she died in 1854 Berlioz married again, this time to a singer named Marie Recio whom he adored, even though he admitted that she sang 'like a cat'.

Throughout his life, Berlioz toured extensively all over Europe, conducting performances of his own and other composers' music despite suffering from a debilitating and painful intestinal condition from 1848 until his death in 1869. However, the unusually large forces required to perform his music meant that the majority of profits were swallowed up by the vast staging costs, and Berlioz had to supplement his income by becoming a music journalist – a job for which he had little enthusiasm.

Berlioz had no interest in adhering to the established musical forms and genres of the day. Form to him was dictated instead by his own impulse and his dramatic instinct. As a result, he invented his own genres for his work, such as the 'dramatic symphony' (*Romeo and Juliet*) and the 'dramatic legend' (*The Damnation of Faust*), the latter lying somewhere between the worlds of opera and oratorio. The last of his three operas, *The Trojans*, was never heard complete in his lifetime and was badly received in its partial performances. Today, however, it is regarded as one of the towering achievements in nineteenth-century opera.

Franz Liszt (1811–1886)

**"My piano... is my very self,
my mother tongue, my life"**

Franz Liszt

Franz Liszt (1811–1886)

Liszt was the archetypal Romantic artist, his life and music both full of contrasting extremes. Europe's most celebrated virtuoso pianist, he had a scandalous love life, yet at the same time he had a deeply contemplative and religious side. Born in a German-speaking area of Hungary, he was a child prodigy. At a very young age, he had the opportunity to play the piano to Beethoven, who was so impressed that he made the uncharacteristically tender gesture of kissing the boy on his forehead. When Liszt was twelve his family moved to Paris, which seemed the obvious place for the boy to develop his talents. Here, he became friends with many of the leading lights in the musical world, such as Berlioz (whose style greatly influenced Listz's own, and to whom his *Faust Symphony* was dedicated), Chopin, and Paganini, the violinist whose virtuoso technique was so astonishing that he was said to be in league with the devil.

This was the age of the virtuoso, and from the very start Liszt's music was characterised by its florid and breathtaking piano writing. Throughout his career he made many astoundingly difficult piano transcriptions of works by other composers, such as Berlioz's *Symphonie fantastique*, Beethoven's symphonies and Schubert's songs.

At the age of twenty-two he met and fell in love with Countess Marie d'Agoult. Marie was already married with two children, but she left her husband for Liszt and had three illegitimate children by him – one of whom, Cosima, would later fall out of favour with her father when she became Wagner's lover. Since his early teens, Liszt had been making concert tours of Europe, accompanied by his father, and before long he enjoyed a celebrity status to rival that of any modern-day pop star. This inevitably brought attention from members of the opposite sex, and all over Europe ladies would swoon and confess their undying love at the very sight of him, which inflamed Marie's inherently and intensely jealous nature. Unfortunately, some of his fans were of a predatory nature, such as the notorious dancer Lola Montez; she forged, primarily for her own social advancement, an intense though short-lived friendship with Liszt which generated a considerable amount of scandalous publicity. (She later became the lover of Ludwig I of Bavaria, her outrageous behaviour very nearly bringing down the Bavarian government.) For Marie, the public humiliation caused by the Lola Montez episode was the straw that broke the camel's back and the pair separated bitterly in 1833, Marie returning to her husband.

When his touring schedule allowed, Liszt would spend as much time as he could in his native Hungary. Displaying a typically Romantic love of folk culture, he would visit gipsy encampments and listen to their wild and exotic music, the influence of which can be heard in Liszt's nineteen Hungarian Rhapsodies.

In 1847 on a trip to Kiev, Liszt fell once again in love with a married woman – Princess Carolyne Sayn-Wittgenstein. This lady, her teeth blackened by years of chain-smoking cigars, did not fit everyone's pre-conceptions of a princess. Despite the Vatican's refusal to grant Princess Carolyne a divorce, the pair moved to Weimar. Liszt gave up his fifteen-year career as a concert pianist and accepted a position as Court Director of Music in which he spent the next ten years promoting new music, conducting and teaching (with characteristic generosity,

At the coronation of Franz Josef I as King of Hungary in 1867, Liszt stole the thunder of the King himself. His electrifying presence was witnessed by one onlooker, Janka Wohl.

An immense crowd of eager sightseers was waiting – on stands, in windows, on the roofs, and in flag-bedecked boats – to see the royal procession which was soon to cross the bridge. When the feverish suspense grew intense, the tall figure of a priest, in a long black cassock studded with decorations, was seen to descend the broad white road leading to the Danube, which had been kept clear for the royal procession. As he walked bareheaded, his snow-white hair floated on the breeze, and his features seemed cast in brass. At his appearance a murmur arose, which swelled and deepened as he advanced and was recognised by the people. The name of Liszt flew down the serried ranks from mouth to mouth, swift as a flash of lightning. Soon a hundred thousand men and women were frantically applauding him, wild with the excitement of this whirlwind of voices. The crowd on the other side of the river naturally thought it must be the King. It was not the King, but it was a king, to whom were addressed the sympathies of a grateful nation proud of the possession of such a son.

he refused to accept any money for the last of these). By this time, he was effectively the head of the progressive 'New German School' of composition, where the musical ideology was much more radical than that of the more conservative composers such as Brahms and Mendelssohn. Those of the New German School encouraged traditional boundaries to be pushed; their music was more chromatic as tonality began to be challenged, and they were less inclined to stick to pre-ordained forms and structures. When Liszt finally gave up all hope of marrying Carolyne, he took minor orders in the Catholic Church and was thereafter known as Abbé Liszt. He spent his remaining twenty years between Rome, Weimar and Budapest. On a trip to Bayreuth in 1886 to visit Wagner and Cosima, with whom he had just about restored reasonable relations, he developed pneumonia and died on 31 July, aged seventy-five.

The most overwhelmingly striking characteristic of Liszt's music is its virtuosity. Unlike Beethoven, whose concertos give largely equal roles to orchestra and soloist, Liszt treats the concerto as an opportunity for the soloist to display technical prowess, for which the orchestra provides a less prominent accompaniment. However, he often combines virtuosity with moments of introspection. This can be heard in the first movement of his Piano Concerto No. 1 website 3 , completed in 1849, in which the breathtaking virtuoso piano passages of the opening are followed by a section of tender beauty (1'56"–3'12"). As he grew older, this tender side to his music came increasingly to the fore, and is particularly audible in the many religious choral works that he wrote after taking holy orders. Like Berlioz, he was a fine orchestrator

Liszt at the piano, 1840, by Josef Danhauser (1804–1845)

*From left: Alexandre Dumas or Alfred de Musset, Victor Hugo,
George Sand, Nicolò Paganini, Gioachino Rossini,
Liszt, Marie d'Agoult; on the piano is a bust of Beethoven*

and based musical form on instinct rather than the existing Classical models. Through works such as *Prometheus* and *Tasso* he effectively invented the symphonic poem – the most sophisticated embodiment of programme music, subsequently taken up by many composers, most notably Tchaikovsky and Richard Strauss. Liszt's detractors have often accused his music of containing nothing more than empty showmanship; but it is much more than that. He was a composer who wrote highly original and finely crafted music which profoundly and directly influenced composers until well into the twentieth century.

Fryderyk Chopin (1810–1849)

Like Liszt, Chopin was another brilliant virtuoso composer–pianist who moved away from his native eastern Europe to the bright lights of Paris. He was born in Warsaw where his father was a schoolmaster of modest means (though sufficiently well enough off to support Chopin into his twenties). By the age of eight, Chopin's precocious composing and piano-playing skills had made him a local celebrity. But as he got older he felt that Warsaw was too restrictive and provincial, and that if he were going to make his mark as a musician he would have to move to a bigger city. In his late teens he made a concert trip to Vienna where he did not go down as well as he had hoped. His virtuoso style was delicate and introverted, and, although his performance there of his own Variations on Mozart's 'Là ci darem la mano' led Schumann to brand him a genius, the general Viennese public preferred more flamboyant celebrities, such as Liszt. The trip was not a resounding success.

Fryderyk Chopin (1810–1849)

"Hats off, gentlemen, a genius!"

Robert Schumann of Chopin

When Russia invaded and conquered Poland in 1831, Chopin made the decision to move to Paris. He was in fact half-French, as his father had been born in Marainville in the east of France and had settled in Warsaw after marrying a Pole. Chopin's first months in France were difficult financially, but before long he had made friends with influential musicians such as Liszt, Rossini and Berlioz, and had built up a good list of aristocratic piano pupils which provided him with a good income for most of his life.

After he had been in Paris for five years, he met and fell in love with the famous female writer George Sand.

> *"I was quite overcome; my heart was conquered...*
> *She understood me... She loves me"*
>
> Chopin of George Sand

George Sand, separated and with two children, had taken a male pen-name and even cross-dressed. She scandalised polite society with her erotic novels, which questioned gender identity and sexual stereotypes. Although she seemed like an unlikely match for a man of such delicate sensibilities as Chopin, she had a tender side and treated him almost like a son at times. They spent the winter of 1838 in Majorca, where Chopin hoped the idyllic setting would enable him to compose in peace; but their accommodation was unsuitable for the harsh winter months and he developed acute chest problems. The trip was a disaster, and almost certainly caused permanent damage to his already fragile immune system. Thereafter Chopin and Sand spent their summers at Sand's estate at Nohant in central France, which she had inherited

from her grandmother in 1821. They were regularly visited by
artistic friends such as the writers Honoré de Balzac and
Heinrich Heine, and the painter Eugène Delacroix, and it
was here that Chopin composed some of his greatest music,
including his twenty-four preludes for piano. By 1847
tensions had appeared in the relationship, caused largely by
the controversial marriage of Sand's daughter Solange to a
sculptor, and Chopin and Sand separated that year. In his
remaining two years Chopin suffered from frequent bouts of
depression and worsening ill-health. In the midst of the 1848
revolution in France, which led to the deposition of the
monarchy, he accepted an invitation to visit England with a
pupil to escape the threatening atmosphere in Paris. But the
change of scene did nothing to relieve his depression and
illness, and after six months he returned to Paris in a much
enfeebled state. His health steadily deteriorated and he died
of tuberculosis the following year, aged only thirty-nine.

You would be forgiven for thinking that the co-existence of
two eastern European piano virtuosi in Paris – Chopin and
Liszt – might lead to rivalry and tension between the men.
However, this was not the case and they remained close
friends until Chopin's death. Chopin's style was much more
introverted than Liszt's and he was much happier giving
concerts in the intimate setting of the salons of his aristocratic
friends, leaving the realm of the concert hall to Liszt. He
never wrote virtuosic music for the sake of virtuosity. For him,
elaborate and florid music served only to emphasise an inner
expression. There were other differences between their music
as well. Chopin had no interest at all in writing programme
music, whereas a large part of Liszt's output was

programmatic. Although Chopin wrote two piano concertos before he left Poland (both inspired by a young woman, Konstancja Gladkowska, with whom he was in love at the time), he is best known for his short piano pieces, such as the preludes, the nocturnes and the études. Much of his piano music, such as the polonaises and mazurkas, was inspired by a love of his native land. The polonaise is a Polish national dance, in which each bar has three beats and often contains a short repeated rhythmic motif. The Polonaise in D minor, Op. 71 No. 1 **website 4** was probably written when Chopin was in his late teens. In it the dance's repeated rhythmic motifs can be heard (e.g. at 0′24″–0′26″ and 2′18–2′20″). The piece has a yearning, melancholic quality common to Polish folk music, indeed to eastern European folk music in general. This quality is typical of Chopin's introverted style, belonging as it did to a melancholic and homesick composer-in-exile.

IV. The Classical Romantics

Franz Schubert (1797–1828)

"Before Schubert's genius we all must bow"

Schubert's friend Johann Michael Vogl

While some composers confidently strode forward into the
new era without so much as a glance over the shoulder at
their predecessors, others were less keen to reject the
traditions of the past. They employed traditional techniques in
their music which showed a reverence for earlier composers
such as Mozart, Haydn and Bach. This didn't mean that they
were in any way *less* Romantic than their more radical
colleagues: their music was still full of intense emotion, and
they developed the established genres in subtle yet important
ways. But their approach had a formality that paid homage to
the music of the Classical and Baroque eras; hence these
composers are known as the 'Classical Romantics'.

Franz Schubert (1797–1828)

Although Schubert was born a generation after Beethoven, he
died only one year after his musical hero. In his short life he
wrote nine symphonies, ten operas, seven masses and a vast
amount of chamber music. However, perhaps his greatest
contribution to musical history was his catalogue of over 600
songs (often referred to by their German name *Lieder*) which
transformed the light-hearted Classical vocal piece into
one of the most sophisticated and deeply felt genres of the
century. It is Schubert's melodic gift that is one of the
hallmarks of his writing. All his music is built from beautiful
and memorable tunes, in contrast to other composers such
as Beethoven, who preferred to create rich musical textures
from short motifs.

Schubert was one of the very few Viennese composers of
the time actually to be born and bred in Vienna. He came

from a modest background: his father was a teacher and his mother a cook. At the age of eleven he went to the Stadtkonvikt, a local boarding school with an excellent reputation for music, and by his final year, when he was sixteen, he had written his first symphony. Although his first six symphonies are very much in the Classical style of Haydn and Mozart, he was writing other works at the same time which were imbued with a true romantic passion.

One of Schubert's most beautiful and enduring songs is *Gretchen am Spinnrade* ('Gretchen at the Spinning Wheel') website 5, written in 1814 when he was just seventeen years old. The text is taken from Goethe's *Faust*: Gretchen, a servant girl, sings of her hopeless infatuation with Faust while she works at the spinning wheel. What sets this song apart from its Classical predecessors is the way in which Schubert elevates the role of the piano from providing mere accompaniment to highlighting and emphasising the meaning of the text. Throughout the song you can hear the piano imitating the repetitive sound and movement of the wheel's treadle. Most of the song is in a sad and desolate minor key; but at 1'18" there is a typically Schubertian key change and we move to the major, as Gretchen describes how proud and handsome Faust looks. She fantasises about holding his hand, and when she imagines kissing him (1'39") the piano stops its repetitive spinning motif, indicating that she is so overcome by the thought that she has stopped working. The moment is brief, however, and we are plunged back into the minor key as Gretchen starts spinning again, remembering that her love is hopeless. Although this song was written early in Schubert's career, it is typical in many ways of his mature style. His late epic song cycle *Die Winterreise* ('The Winter Journey') is based on a similarly Romantic theme of hopeless love: a poet wandering alone in a bleak landscape having been rejected by his lover. The majority of *Winterreise* is also in minor keys, moving to happier major ones only on a few occasions when the poet is either dreaming or suffering delusions.

When Schubert left the Stadtkonvikt, he worked for a few years as a junior teacher in his father's school. He hated it, but it helped him to finance composition lessons from Salieri. Schubert lived in poverty throughout his life, relying on the generosity of friends to get by. It was a rich law student named Franz von Schober who enabled him to leave his teaching job by offering him a free roof over his head and the chance to concentrate solely on his composition. Lucrative commissions were only available in those days to composers who, unlike Schubert, moved in the close-knit circles of the musical establishment. Although his late symphonies broke new ground in terms of harmonic language, employing unprecedented and striking key changes, No. 9 (the 'Great') was not premiered until eleven years after his death, and No. 8 (the 'Unfinished') not until a quarter of a century after that. Vienna was not as wealthy as it had been in the previous century, and the middle classes took to organising private chamber music concerts in their salons as a relatively inexpensive form of musical entertainment. Schubert's friends organised many such concerts, for which much of his music was written, and these became known as 'Schubertiads'.

In 1818 Schubert received the only official appointment of his lifetime, as music master to the family of Count Esterházy.

For two summers, Schubert left Vienna behind and taught the Count's two daughters in the very pleasant surroundings at the Esterházy estate in Zseliz, Hungary. It seems likely that it was on one of these summers that Schubert contracted syphilis, possibly from a servant girl, which was the cause of much suffering in his final years. Ironically, it was a recurrence of his symptoms that led Schubert's doctor to recommend that he go to the newer suburbs of Vienna to recuperate; here the lack of decent plumbing led him to contract typhus, the probable cause of his early death.

Felix Mendelssohn (1809–1847)

There are many parallels between the lives and works of Schubert and Mendelssohn: both were child prodigies, both had a great melodic gift, and both died tragically young. However, unlike Schubert, Mendelssohn enjoyed financial stability and happy, secure personal circumstances throughout his life. His grandfather Moses Mendelssohn was a famous philosopher, and his father was a well-off Jewish banker who, due to the ominous increase in anti-Semitism in early-nineteenth-century Europe, converted to the Protestant Church and changed the family name to the more Aryan-sounding Mendelssohn-Bartholdy.

Born in Hamburg, Mendelssohn was taught the piano at an early age by his mother and went on to study harmony and music theory with Carl Friedrich Zelter. Zelter instilled in Mendelssohn a great love of the music of Mozart and Bach, which was to be an important influence on his own work. In fact, Mendelssohn was largely responsible for bringing

Felix Mendelssohn (1809–1847)

"The Mozart of the 19th century"

Robert Schumann about Mendelssohn

Bach's music, which had been neglected for over a century, to public attention: he staged the first performance of the St Matthew Passion since Bach's death.

From an early age Mendelssohn was a prolific composer. By the time he left school he was already boasting a large catalogue of works, including thirteen string symphonies as well as his enchanting overture *A Midsummer Night's Dream*. He toured extensively as a pianist and was particularly well received in England, where he regularly enjoyed musical soirées with Queen Victoria and Prince Albert. In 1829 he also made a trip to Scotland – a country romanticised by the novels of Sir Walter Scott – where he wrote his famous overture *The Hebrides* and started work on his Symphony No. 3. This was subtitled 'The Scottish', and included a musical depiction of a visit to Edinburgh's Holyrood Palace.

The Hebrides ⟨website 6 ⟩, which has also been known as 'The Lonesome Isle', 'The Isles of Fingal' and 'Fingal's Cave', was inspired by a visit to the Hebridean island of Staffa, a journey that made Mendelssohn horribly seasick, so legend has it. Although the layout of the overture stays within sonata form (the sophisticated structure developed in the Classical era), it adheres to the Romantic notion of programme music in its depiction of a non-musical idea; indeed the flowing lyricism of the piece could only be a product of the nineteenth century. Throughout the work, the music eloquently evokes the grey Scottish skies and movement of the sea. At 0'21" you can hear the lower strings imitating the rippling water, whereas at 1'53" the upper strings seem to suggest a calmer sea shimmering in the daylight.

Mendelssohn visited Fingal's Cave on the island of Staffa on 7 August 1829. His travelling companion, Karl Klingemann, wrote the following account of the visit:

Staffa, with its strange basalt pillars and caverns, is in all the picture books. We were put out in boats and lifted by the hissing sea up the pillar stumps to the famous Fingal's Cave. A greener roar of waves never rushed into a stranger cavern – its many pillars making it look like the inside of an immense organ, black and resounding, absolutely without purpose, and quite alone, the wide grey sea within and without.

In 1835 Mendelssohn moved to Leipzig where he took over artistic directorship of the Leipzig Gewandhaus Orchestra, transforming it into one of the greatest orchestras in Europe, a reputation which the orchestra maintains today. Two years later, he married Cécile Jeanrenaud, the daughter of a minister of the French Reformed Church, and the pair enjoyed a happy marriage and had five children during their ten years together. With Robert Schumann, Mendelssohn set up the Leipzig Conservatory of Music in 1842 and added piano teaching to his already packed schedule of conducting and playing, both in Leipzig and on tour. When he heard in 1847 that his beloved sister Fanny had suffered a stroke, the pressure became too much and he too had a stroke. He spent some time recuperating in Switzerland, but when he returned to work in Leipzig he had a second stroke and eventually died on 4 November 1847, aged only thirty-eight.

Posterity has not always been kind to Mendelssohn's music. He has often been referred to in disparaging tones as an arch-conservative. His love of Bach and Mozart, and strict musical techniques such as fugue and counterpoint, led Berlioz to comment that he 'studied the music of the dead rather too much'. In 1849 Wagner published (anonymously) a poisonously anti-Semitic article entitled 'Jewishness in Music' directed largely against Mendelssohn, and almost a century later Mendelssohn's music was banned by the Nazis. He may not have expressed the extremity of passion that Liszt did, but his writing was innovative and inspired at the same time, and he left important works in every genre except opera. His much-loved *Songs without Words* developed the Romantic fashion for short, character pieces for piano; his

Violin Concerto, one of the greatest ever written, demonstrates the Romantic ideal of unity in a work of art; the piece is played without a break as its three movements run straight into each other. Today, fortunately, there is a general recognition of Mendelssohn's genius and an appreciation of his invaluable contribution to musical history.

Robert Schumann (1810–1856)

Robert Schumann was born in Zwickau in Saxony. His mother's ambition was that he should become a lawyer, and following her wishes he embarked on a law course in Leipzig when he was eighteen. However, his artistic instincts proved too strong and he gave up law to dedicate his energies to music, much to his mother's dismay. He took up lodgings with his music teacher Friedrich Wieck, who had partially appeased Frau Schumann by a somewhat ambitious assurance that he would transform her son into one of the greatest pianists in Europe. Schumann's promising career as a pianist, however, was thwarted by paralysis in one of his fingers, which seems to have been caused by his overuse of a specially made machine designed to strengthen his fourth finger.

It was while he was living with Wieck that Schumann became engaged to Ernestine von Fricken, another of Wieck's pupils. However, the essentially conservative Robert broke off the engagement in 1834 when he found out that Ernestine was illegitimate; he transferred his amorous attentions onto Wieck's daughter Clara, much to the horror of her father. For

Robert Schumann (1810–1856)

"To me, Schumann's memory is holy"

Johannes Brahms

the next six years Wieck did his best to keep the couple apart, during which time Schumann wrote many short pieces for solo piano. In some of these he liked to use hidden codes to refer to extra-musical themes. For example, his Fantasie in C major, Op. 17 quotes from a song by Beethoven, *An die ferne Geliebte* ('To the Distant Beloved'), suggesting the pain he felt over his separation from Clara.

After winning an acrimonious lawsuit to overturn Wieck's earlier legal blocking of their union, Robert and Clara eventually got married in 1840. Clara was an extremely talented pianist – she was to become one of the greatest in Europe. She also had ambitions to be a composer, but Robert, as his treatment of Ernestine von Fricken had shown, was a traditional character and he strongly discouraged this, presumably worried about a challenge to his position as head of the household. At this point he turned his attention from solo piano music to song writing. In the year of his marriage he wrote almost 150 songs, the texts of which are mostly about blissful love. Schumann was the natural heir to Schubert in this field, and much of his most successful music dates from this year, such as the song cycles *Dichterliebe* ('Poet's Love') and *Frauenliebe und -leben* ('A Woman's Love and Life').

It is an interesting quirk of Schumann's career that he tended to concentrate, generally speaking, on one genre at a time. After his song-writing year in 1840 he threw himself into composing symphonic music, which was followed by phases of chamber music, then oratorio, dramatic music (he composed one opera, *Genoveva*, but it was not a success), and finally church music. Schumann's music is often programmatic – the fourth movement of his Third Symphony 'Rhenish' is a depiction of Cologne Cathedral. However, he was reluctant to give movements specific programmatic titles as he believed that doing so restricted the scope of a listener's individual response to the music. Although his four symphonies are based on the Classical model of the previous century, he made further innovations in terms of form and developed the concept of making the symphony a unified whole instead of four separate movements. All the movements, for example, in his Fourth Symphony (as in Mendelssohn's Violin Concerto) run directly into one another, the work being played without a break.

Elements of both his forward-looking and traditional tendencies can be heard in the exciting final movement of his Piano Quintet in E flat , written in 1843. In the minute-long section beginning at 5'21", Schumann writes a fugue – music in which all the parts weave a formalised tapestry with overlapping statements of a theme. This was a complex technique which had had its heyday in Bach's time, over a century before. The theme Schumann uses for his fugue is the main theme of the quintet's first movement. The use of the same material across different movements of a piece was a new idea in the nineteenth century: in this case it inextricably links the very beginning and end of the quintet, providing a feeling of unity throughout the work. Clara loved this quintet and kept it in her repertoire for the rest of her performing career, although Robert criticised her performance of it, proclaiming that only a man could understand the music properly. Liszt, on the other hand, as head of the radical 'New German School', greatly offended

Schumann by claiming that the work was too conservative and reminiscent of Mendelssohn.

Schumann was also a well-known music critic. In fact, he was probably better known as a critic than a composer during his lifetime. In 1834 he founded an influential music journal called the *Neue Zeitschrift für Musik* and during his ten years as editor did much to promote the works of fellow composers such as Berlioz, Mendelssohn, Chopin and Brahms. Brahms, as we shall see, was to become a close family friend: he did much to help Clara in affairs of household management when the deterioration of Robert's physical and mental health due to syphilis became severe. The first signs of illness were evident as early as 1846. By 1854 Schumman's mental faculties had left him altogether, and, after he tried unsuccessfully to commit suicide by throwing himself into the Rhein, he was committed to an asylum where he spent the remaining two wretched years of his life.

Johannes Brahms (1833–1897)

Brahms was born and brought up in a seedy and impoverished part of Hamburg. His father was a double-bass player and his mother a seamstress, and as such they had very little money. By the time Brahms was in his teens he was earning his keep by playing the piano in the local 'dockside taverns', which in reality were little more than brothels. Later in life, Brahms claimed that the scenes he witnessed in these taverns tainted his attitude towards sexual relationships and were the primary reason why he himself never settled down.

Johannes Brahms (1833–1897)

**"Here is one who seems to have come
straight from God"**

Clara Schumann, on first hearing Brahms play the piano

However, it was in one of these taverns that the exiled Hungarian violinist Eduard Reményi met Brahms and gave him his first important break. Reményi was so impressed with the young Brahms's piano playing that he invited him on tour as his accompanist. Their artistic collaboration did not last long, and they parted company when Reményi became disgruntled that his brilliant young accompanist was attracting more attention than he was. But he did introduce Brahms to the world-famous violinist Joseph Joachim, who was to become a lifelong friend and who in turn introduced him to Robert and Clara Schumann. The Schumanns were bowled over when Brahms played them his compositions and they immediately took him under their wing. With the characteristic generosity he showed talented young musicians, Schumann wrote glowing reports about him in the influential *Neue Zeitschrift für Musik*. After Schumann's failed suicide attempt in 1854, Brahms moved into the family home and was immensely supportive to Clara and her children. It was a thinly disguised secret that Brahms had been passionately in love with Clara ever since he met her, and she too was devoted to him. Although there is no evidence that anything happened between them, Clara's jealousy when Brahms became engaged to another woman in 1858 suggests that her devotion may also have been of a romantic nature. Brahms broke off his engagement the following year, claiming he did not want to be tied down, and enjoyed a close, though sometimes turbulent, friendship with Clara until her death in 1896.

In the early part of his career, Brahms's output comprised almost exclusively chamber music. Beethoven, his hero, had

When the twenty-year-old Brahms was first introduced to Robert and Clara Schumann by his friend Joseph Joachim, he played the piano to them. Following the meeting, Clara wrote down her impressions:

He played us sonatas, scherzos, and other pieces, all his own, each showing the most exuberant imagination, depth of feeling, and mastery of form. Robert says that there was nothing he could tell him to take away or to add. It is really very moving to see him sitting at the piano, with his interesting young face, which becomes transfigured when he plays, his beautiful hands, which overcome the most fearsome difficulties with perfect ease (his things are very difficult), and in addition, these remarkable compositions. He has studied with Marxsen in Hamburg, but what he played to us is so masterly that one can only believe that the good God sent him into the world ready-made. He has a great future ahead of him, for he will first find the true field for his genius when he begins to write for the orchestra. Robert says there is nothing to wish except that heaven preserve his health.

left behind such a monumental legacy of symphonic music that Brahms was terrified of writing orchestral music. 'You have no idea how it feels to a man like me to have a giant like Beethoven marching behind,' he once said, and he was well into his forties before his First Symphony appeared. He did, however, produce his First Piano Concerto when he was twenty-six. Although it was Classical in form, no earlier piano concerto had come close to its grand scale and level of emotional intensity. Today it is acknowledged as one of the greatest concertos ever written, but the sheer size of the work and the density of its musical argument were too much for the audience at the premiere and it was panned by the critics. When his First Symphony finally appeared in 1876, it achieved a more favourable critical reaction, though some snidely dubbed it 'Beethoven's Tenth' due to a tenuous similarity between the main theme of its first movement and that of the last movement of Beethoven's Ninth.

Brahms as a young man had been beautiful, with piercing eyes and an innocent expression; but as he became older, he became increasingly scruffy and grumpy. He would regularly make cutting and sarcastic comments, and so alienated many of his good friends. This bitter demeanour was perhaps not surprising given the circumstances of his life: his upbringing in poverty, the often bad critical reception of his work, and his lack of success in love. He also suffered several major public humiliations. On two occasions he applied to be Principal Conductor of the Hamburg Philharmonic, only to be rejected both times in favour of a less talented candidate. Moreover, he once wrote an extremely sour and ill-advised letter to the *Neue Zeitschrift für Musik* railing against the proponents of Liszt's New German School of composition. He had intended for the letter to be signed by many distinguished musicians, but for reasons that remain unexplained it was printed prematurely, signed only by himself, Joachim and two musical non-entities: it made Brahms the laughing-stock of the music world. Yet beneath the tough exterior of this old curmudgeon lay a deeply sensitive, innocent and generous soul who, right up until his death of liver cancer in 1897, loved walking in the countryside, laughing and playing with children, and collecting toy soldiers. He also willingly bailed friends out of financial difficulties.

The contrasting aspects of Brahms's personality are mirrored by a juxtaposition of conservatism and heart-breaking poignancy in his musical style. In his Intermezzo in A major, Op. 118 No. 2 for solo piano (website 8), the middle section consists of a tune which is played three times in different guises: first with lyrical beauty at 1'48"; repeated at 2'27" in a formal-sounding manner, almost reminiscent of a Bach chorale; then it is heard a third time imbued with a moving and passionate intensity, before a reprieve of the enchanting opening section draws this short piece to a close.

V. Opera in the Nineteenth Century

Gioachino Rossini (1792–1868)

"Give me a laundry list, and I will set it to music"

Gioachino Rossini

Although Paris was arguably the greatest operatic centre in Europe throughout the nineteenth century, the quality of opera being produced by French composers was, frankly, fairly low. There were many French 'grands opéras' which used huge orchestras and choruses, and sought any excuse for all kinds of spectacle, but they tended to lack severely in musical and dramatic substance. Of course there were exceptions: Berlioz, as mentioned earlier, made some extremely important additions to the operatic repertoire; and Bizet's *Carmen* is an undisputed masterpiece. But to examine the most important trends in Romantic opera, we need to look at what was happening in Italy and Germany. These two countries had very different approaches to opera and there was a strong rivalry between the two traditions, highlighted by Rossini's famous comment about his distinguished German colleague: 'Wagner is a composer who has beautiful moments, but awful half hours'.

Italian Opera

Italian opera composers at the beginning of the nineteenth century inherited a tradition of vocal writing known as *bel canto* – 'beautiful singing' – in which more emphasis was placed on fine phrasing, technique and beauty of tone than on dramatic concerns. Opera composers in the previous century had been largely expected to provide soloists with a stage exit at the end of each aria (and less than two arias per soloist per act would be regarded as a snub) in order that the singers could make a prominent re-entrance for the sole purpose of receiving their tumultuous applause.

Gioachino Rossini (1792–1868)

Rossini was the first major figure to inject some gravitas into the Italian operatic tradition. In the early part of his career he tended to concentrate on *opera buffa*, or comic opera. With works such as *The Italian Girl in Algiers* (1813) and *The Barber of Seville* (1816) he quickly developed celebrity status throughout Europe. Nowhere is his distinctive *bel canto* style more evident than in the florid vocal lines of the wonderfully infectious aria 'Nacqui all'affanno e al pianto' ⟨website 9⟩ from his opera *La Cenerentola* ('Cinderella'). This aria appears at the end of the opera, and in it Cinderella forgives her family for their cruelty, saying that her many years of suffering seem like a dream now that the Prince has swept her off her feet. Between 3'46" and 4'15" there is an example of the famous 'Rossini crescendo', in which the composer gradually builds up to a climax by increasing the texture and volume of the music over a repeating phrase.

In 1815 he moved to Naples at the invitation of impresario Domenico Barbaia, who wanted him to revitalise the operatic tradition in the theatres there. From this time, he turned his attention to *opera seria*, or serious opera, developing the genre by giving the chorus a more dramatic role in the action, writing for larger orchestras, and using reminiscence motifs (recurring themes attributed to a particular character).

In 1823 he made another move, this time to Paris, where he had been appointed Artistic Director of the Théâtre Italien; it was there that he wrote his greatest serious opera, *William Tell*, in 1828. It was the last opera he wrote, and in 1837, having secured a generous and unconditional annuity from the French State, he retired and moved back to Italy to spend the remaining forty years of his life.

Vincenzo Bellini (1801–1835)
Gaetano Donizetti (1797–1848)

With the development of *opera seria* these two composers took over where Rossini had left off. In the late eighteenth and early nineteenth centuries, *opera seria* had almost always ended happily. However, Bellini and Donizetti started a trend for tragic endings which invariably involved the leading lady dying for love in the final scene. Bellini's *Norma*, first performed at La Scala in Milan in 1831, is the first great example of this approach. These tragic heroines would often lose their minds before they died, and a 'mad scene' became a common phenomenon in operas of this type, providing scope for composers to use the *bel canto* tradition to powerfully dramatic, instead of primarily ostentatious, effect.

One of the most famous operatic mad scenes in the repertoire comes from Donizetti's *Lucia di Lammermoor* (produced in 1835). Based on a novel by Sir Walter Scott, it is set at Lucia's wedding banquet. She has been forced by her brother Enrico to marry against her will, and to forget her beloved Edgardo, Enrico's deadliest enemy. The scene begins immediately after the guests learn that Lucia has gone mad and killed her husband. She appears, to everyone's horror, in a blood-stained gown, hallucinating that she is sitting by a fountain with Edgardo on the morning of *their* wedding, pledging her fidelity to him. Her deranged state of mind is depicted by the contrast of moods and disjointedness of the music she sings. The scene reaches a climax with her aria 'Spargi d'amaro pianto' (website 10), in which she tells Edgardo (whose presence she is merely imagining) that she is dying, and that while he should cry for her on earth they will one

Gaetano Donizetti (1797–1848)

day be happy together in heaven. On the surface the music might sound light-hearted; but in the context of her delusion, her reflections on her own death, and the strangely slower-than-expected tempo, the bright and florid vocal line creates a dark and chilling effect.

Giuseppe Verdi (1813–1901)

Verdi was without doubt the towering figure in Italian opera in the nineteenth century. He was born into a family of modest means near the town of Busseto, near Parma. He left the family home before he reached his teens to go and live with a rich patron, Antonio Barezzi. When he was twenty-three, he married Barezzi's daughter and they had two children: a boy and a girl. But, with tragic irony, his wife and both their children died around the time that Verdi was working on a comic opera, *Un giorno di regno* ('King for a Day'). The opera was a disaster and Verdi nearly gave up composition altogether. However, he persevered, and when *Nabucco* appeared in 1842 it was a triumph, turning Verdi almost overnight into a national hero. Aside from the quality of the music, one of the reasons that this work earned Verdi cult status was the subject matter, which dealt with the Babylonian enslavement of the Hebrews. This touched a deep chord within the collective consciousness of the Italian people, who themselves were struggling for political independence, and the famous Chorus of the Hebrew Slaves from the opera became something of an unofficial national anthem. Five years later, the Chorus of the Scottish Exiles from his opera *Macbeth* had a similar effect. *Macbeth*

Giuseppe Verdi (1813–1901)

**"It is a good thing to copy reality;
but to invent reality is much, much better"**

Giuseppe Verdi

represented a landmark in Italian opera. Here, it was clear that Verdi was beginning to break away from the firmly established *bel canto* tradition and place more emphasis on realistic drama than purely beautiful singing. He actually specified that Lady Macbeth should *not* have a beautiful voice and that her sleepwalking scene should 'on no account be sung, but declaimed with the voice dark and veiled' (see page 70).

Verdi's popularity as a national symbol increased over the years, and in the 1860s his name started to be used as a political slogan: it was discovered that it could stand for '**V**ittorio **E**manuele, **R**e **d'I**talia' ('Vittorio Emanuele, King of Italy'), Vittorio Emanuele being the most popular candidate for monarch of the independent country that the Italians were fighting for. However, throughout his life Verdi was a reluctant public figure on both the political and musical scenes, and he was at his happiest when he was tending the garden in his country estate at St Agata, near Busseto. He bought the estate in 1851 with his partner, the soprano Giuseppina Strepponi, whom he eventually married in 1859.

Verdi continued to develop the concept of dramatic characterisation, and by the time *Rigoletto* appeared in 1851 it was clear that he had elevated 'grand opera' to a new level, far removed from its superficial beginnings on the Parisian stage half a century before. He continued to produce masterpiece after masterpiece with works such as *Il trovatore*, *La traviata*, *Don Carlos* and *Aida*. These works were showing a tendency to be more seamless than their predecessors, which reflected the Romantic propensity of making a piece of music as unified as possible throughout. Earlier operas had

In a famous letter, Verdi's views on the interpretation of the role of Lady Macbeth were in direct opposition to the bel canto tradition:

I am given to understand that Mme Tadolini is to sing Lady Macbeth. I am frankly astonished that she should have undertaken this role. It is well known that I admire Mme Tadolini greatly. She knows this too. But in the interests of all, I must point out that her qualities are too great for this part – however absurd such a declaration may seem! Mme Tadolini is beautiful and of a virtuous appearance, whereas Lady Macbeth should be ugly and conspicuously evil. Mme Tadolini sings to perfection; ideally I should prefer not to have Lady Macbeth sing at all. Mme Tadolini has a wonderful voice, clear, caressing and strong. Lady Macbeth should sound hard, comfortless and dark. Mme Tadolini's voice is that of an angel, while Lady Macbeth's should be the voice of a demon.

traditionally been split up into separate numbers – arias, choruses, ensembles – which were interspersed by sections of recitative, in which the words would be sung in a declamatory fashion with minimal accompaniment. But in the works Verdi was writing in the 1850s and 1860s, the joins between the numbers were becoming more fluid, and the 'in-between' sections, such as recitative, were becoming musically as refined as the ensembles and arias.

When studying the vast developments that Verdi made in the field of opera, it is easy to get bogged down in a dry discussion of technical matters and lose sight of the fact that his popular appeal is due largely to his talent for writing great tunes. So now may be the perfect time to take a break and listen to one of them. 'È lui… Dio che nell'alma infondere' (website 11) is a tenor and baritone duet which appears in Act II of *Don Carlos*. In it, the eponymous hero – the son of King Philip II of Spain – admits to his friend the Marquis of Posa that he is in love with his father's wife. The main tune of this duet is a reminiscence motif that appears throughout the opera, representing the eternal friendship of these two characters.

In Verdi's last two operas he returned to Shakespeare, beloved of so many Romantic artists. *Otello* and *Falstaff*, both of which were premiered at La Scala in Milan, are the most seamless of all his operas, the breaks between the numbers now being almost undetectable. This, together with the extremely sophisticated characterisation and word-setting in these works, led many to dub him the 'Wagner of Italy'. (Unfortunately, such was the rivalry between the German and Italian operatic traditions that Verdi regarded this as an insult.) The comic story of *Falstaff* was a surprising choice for a composer who had concentrated on the tragic *opera seria* for the majority of his career; yet, written when he was in his late seventies, it is as exuberant and youthful-sounding as you could imagine. Verdi lived for another eight years after the premiere of *Falstaff*, finally succumbing to a fatal stroke in 1901 at St Agata, at the age of eighty-eight.

German Opera

There was not much in the way of a German operatic tradition before the nineteenth century. The two significant German operas were written by Mozart – *Die Entführung aus dem Serail* ('The Abduction from the Seraglio') and *Die Zauberflöte* ('The Magic Flute') – but, despite the fact that he was a native German speaker, the rest of Mozart's operas were in Italian. The main difference between German and Italian opera was that the German variety used spoken dialogue for the sections in which the plot moves forward, whereas the Italian used sung recitative.

Carl Maria von Weber (1786–1826)

Weber fulfilled a similar role in Germany to that of Rossini in Italy: dragging opera into the Romantic era and establishing a high standard on which future composers could build. His most influential work was *Der Freischütz* ('The Marksman'), which was first performed in 1821. It was based on a story which embodied many elements inherent in the Romantic spirit, such as the supernatural, and folk-like scenes which

Carl Maria von Weber (1786–1826)

**"Weber must write operas now; nothing
but operas, one after another"**

Ludwig van Beethoven

glorified peasant life. Of particular importance was his sophisticated use of the reminiscence motif, which was often heard in the orchestral accompaniment where it enhanced the psychological aspect of the drama. This is a technique that Wagner would pick up and develop to an extent that no one could have predicted.

Richard Wagner (1813–1883)

Wagner did more than any other Romantic composer, besides Beethoven, to change the face of western classical music. He was responsible for huge developments in every aspect of music, including harmony, rhythm, melody, orchestration, form and text. His innovations stretched the Romantic ideal to its limit, and in many ways his work was the catalyst which led music away from the Romantic era and into the twentieth century.

He was born in Leipzig, where he went on to study music at university. During his twenties he accrued some considerable debts, and in 1839 he slipped away to Paris with his first wife Minna Planer to Paris in order to escape his creditors. He spent three years there, soaking up all that was happening on the opera scene. He returned to Germany in 1842, but only for five years, as he was involved in the political uprising in Dresden in 1848 and had to flee to Switzerland (aided by Liszt) to escape arrest and imprisonment. He lived there as an exile until he was granted amnesty eleven years later. In 1862 he returned to Germany, settling in Munich, where he fell in love with Cosima von Bülow, Liszt's daughter. She was married at

Richard Wagner (1813–1883)

**"If one has not heard Wagner at Bayreuth,
one has heard nothing"**

Gabriel Fauré, 1884

this time to the great conductor Hans von Bülow, but he, surprisingly, condoned the affair and she eventually became Wagner's second wife in 1870.

From the start of his career, Wagner had a vision of creating a *Gesamtkunstwerk* ('total work of art') – the ultimate specimen of the unified art form. He also referred to this concept as *Zukunftsmusik* or 'music of the future'. In it, music, literature, painting and drama would all fuse into one entity, in which all elements were of equal importance. Not only would all the different art forms become integrated, but the natural, supernatural and human worlds would all begin to merge as well. An early example of this can be seen in his first major opera, *The Flying Dutchman* – it tells the story of a mythical Dutch sea captain, condemned to sail the oceans alone for eternity unless he can find the love of a maiden to set him free from the curse. The storm music, which introduces Act I, mirrors the psychological state of the Dutchman, setting the mood for the whole piece.

In *The Flying Dutchman*, as well as his next two operas *Tannhäuser* and *Lohengrin* (both based on Arthurian legend), individual musical numbers are still in evidence to some degree; but by the time Wagner came to write his monumental cycle of operas *Der Ring des Nibelungen*, this sectional approach had disappeared completely. The *Ring* cycle is one of the most astounding achievements in the history of music. It comprises four operas – *Das Rheingold*, *Die Walküre*, *Siegfried* and *Götterdämmerung* – and totals approximately eighteen hours of music. The text is based on various Norse and Germanic mythological sources and was written by Wagner himself (he was his own librettist for all his operas). The story could be described as a nineteenth-century version of *The Lord of the Rings*: the Gods are on the verge of destruction, and all races are battling to win the Ring forged from gold from the bed of the Rhine, as it will bring power over the Universe to its owner. In the *Ring*, the merging together of the natural and supernatural worlds is more subtly developed than in Wagner's earlier works: Loge, the God of Fire, for example, is both man and element, appearing as a human in *Das Rheingold* but as a circle of fire in the subsequent operas.

The *Ring* cycle is built on literally hundreds of 'leitmotifs' – Wagner's highly developed version of the reminiscence motif. Leitmotifs do not simply appear whenever a character pops up on stage, but are used within the orchestral texture to comment on and heighten the psychological drama, and carry the action. For example, in *Das Rheingold*, the giants Fasolt and Fafner discuss whether they would rather receive the goddess Freia or the Rhinegold as a reward for building the castle Valhalla for the Gods. Initially, when they consider Freia the better prize, her leitmotif is heard in the orchestra; but as they change their minds it slips away to the lower instruments, and the Rhinegold motif assumes prominence.

For Wagner, it was not enough just to write this ground-breaking cycle of operas: he also wanted a special new theatre in which to perform them. So King Ludwig II of Bavaria, who had bailed him out of financial difficulties before, paid for the building of the theatre at Bayreuth. It was there that the first complete performance of the four operas of the *Ring* cycle was given in 1876. The most significant innovation of this theatre was its covered orchestral pit, which created an excellent acoustic by ensuring that the singers were not drowned out by Wagner's vast orchestra. The theatre is still run by the Wagner family today, and is home to an annual festival of Wagner's music.

While he was approximately halfway through writing the *Ring* cycle, Wagner interrupted his work to embark on a new opera. *Tristan and Isolde* (1859), based on a Celtic myth, is in many ways the ultimate love story, one in which love is so powerful and all-encompassing that it can only reach fulfilment in death. Even more so than the operas in the *Ring*, *Tristan* is written as one continuous entity: not only is there an absence of individual musical numbers, but there are virtually no breaks between musical phrases throughout the work, the melodic style being one which Wagner described as 'unendliche Melodie' ('unending melody'). The Prelude to *Tristan and Isolde* (website 12) builds up in just seven minutes a musical picture of this love's almost unbearably intense yearning. At the beginning there is a chord, heard first at 0'07", which has become known as the 'Tristan' chord (see pages 158–9). Musicologists have argued for almost 150 years about the harmonic implications of this chord, and have never reached a conclusion. And here lies the reason why *Tristan and Isolde* shook the entire precept of western music to the core: for the first time in musical history it was impossible to tell what key the music was in. This was the first step in the rejection of tonality (the idea of music being 'in a key') as a basis for composition, a rejection which would eventually herald the end of the Romantic era and the dawn of the twentieth century in music.

A sketch of the end of Wagner's Prelude to
Tristan and Isolde *in the composer's own hand*

As Verdi had unpredictably written a comic opera at the end of his career, so did Wagner surprise the music world with *Die Meistersinger von Nürnberg*. After the unprecedented intensity of the *Ring* and *Tristan and Isolde*, here was an opera which was basically an ingenious comic review of 150 years of German music. Gone is the highly developed seamless style, and instead *Die Meistersinger* is split into individual arias, ensembles and choruses, including some bitingly satirical caricatures of well-known figures of the day – such as the critic Eduard Hanslick, a close friend of Brahms, and chief opponent of the 'New German School' to which Wagner firmly belonged.

For his final opera *Parsifal* he returned to Arthurian legend and produced another epic work, almost more of a religious celebration than a conventional opera. It was first performed at Bayreuth in 1882, the year before Wagner died having suffering a series of heart attacks.

Wagner can be an uncomfortable and confusing character to judge. He held some strongly anti-Semitic views, and many of his critics claim that the *Ring* cycle is founded upon a belief in the supremacy of racial purity. On the other hand, he had a vision of a unified world in which everyone is equal. In an essay on Beethoven dating from 1870, he wrote that 'the language of tones belongs equally to all mankind, and melody is the absolute language in which the musician speaks to every heart'. This stands in direct contrast to the unsavoury opinions expressed in his article entitled *Jewishness in Music*, published in 1849. But the lives of all great revolutionaries are filled with paradox and controversy, and whatever your views on the man his contribution to western music can never be underestimated.

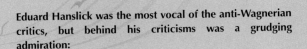

Eduard Hanslick was the most vocal of the anti-Wagnerian critics, but behind his criticisms was a grudging admiration:

I know very well that Wagner is the greatest living composer of opera, and in a historical sense the only one worth talking about... But when art enters a period of luxury, it is already on the decline. Wagner's operatic style recognises only superlatives, and a superlative has no future. It is an end, not a beginning... One could say of this tone poetry: There is music in it – but it is not music.

VI. The Nationalists

Mikhail Ivanovich Glinka (1804–1857)

"I should like to unite in legitimate bonds, the Russian popular song with the good old western fugue"

Mikhail Ivanovich Glinka, on his opera *A Life for the Tsar*

We have already seen how some composers used music to express their sense of national identity: Chopin wrote piano pieces based on Polish dance forms, such as the polonaise; Verdi tapped into the political consciousness of the Italian people with the subject matter of his operas; and, drawing on Germanic mythology, Wagner aimed to create an art form that was specifically German.

This trend for 'nationalist' music became particularly strong in the second half of the nineteenth century – especially among composers from eastern Europe – and it manifested itself primarily in composers' use of traditional folk music in their works for the concert hall. Revolutions spread throughout Europe in 1848 as people kicked back against the domination of foreign powers. Since the beginning of the century, frequent Napoleonic invasions, as well as the tight control held over substantial parts of Europe by the Austrian Empire, had challenged many nations' sense of identity. People began to celebrate their national languages and traditions as a form of passive resistance. The increased interest in national culture was also a result of the cosmopolitanism found in many major European cities. Artists came into contact with the culture and traditions of different countries on a daily basis. This caused them to examine their own indigenous folk culture, and, finding that it was an important factor in both national identity and self-definition, they used it in their work as expressive means.

Russia

Until the nineteenth century, Russia had been largely isolated culturally from the rest of Europe. Its affiliation to the

Orthodox, as opposed to the Catholic, Church meant that it belonged more to the East than to the West. As such, there is a noticeable absence of significant Russian composers before 1830. **Mikhail Ivanovich Glinka** (1804–1857) is regarded as the 'father of Russian music'. His two operas, *A Life for the Tsar* and *Ruslan and Lyudmila*, were extremely popular in his lifetime; in them he combined the techniques he had studied in Germany and Italy with traditional Russian folksong and distinctly Russian plots. In his orchestral work *Kamarinskaya* ꬵwebsite 15 ꬵ he brilliantly developed a special musical technique of continually repeating a short, simple folk tune against an ever-changing accompaniment. This technique closely mirrored the perpetual repetition of melodic motifs in Russian folksong.

Glinka was the inspiration for a new generation of Russian composers. At the beginning of the second half of the century, five of them formed a group to promote Russian nationalism in music. The composers were **Mily Balakirev** (1837–1910), **César Cui** (1835–1918), **Alexander Borodin** (1833–1887), **Modest Mussorgsky** (1839–1881) and **Nikolai Rimsky-Korsakov** (1844–1908) – and collectively they became known as 'The Five', or 'The Mighty Handful'. With their combined skills they supported each other in different aspects of their work: for example, Mussorgsky would help Rimsky-Korskov refine his recitative, and in return Rimsky-Korsakov helped Mussorgsky with his harmonies. At one point, the Imperial Russian Opera suggested that all five jointly write an opera, *Mlada*. They started work on it, but the opera was never performed whole as intended, and the composers ended up adapting what they had written for use in other pieces.

Balakirev was the most charismatic of the five and he effectively led the group, though his music is rarely heard in the concert hall today. He was the only professional musician among them: Borodin was an eminent chemist and the other three had military careers. Cui was the first to join Balakirev's set, and he spent a good deal of time writing articles praising the friends and criticising the opponents of Russian musical nationalism. Surprisingly, however, there seems to be very little influence of Russian folk music in his own works, which have stood the test of time less successfully than even Balakirev's.

Borodin had little formal training in music (a common problem among Russian composers of the time), though Balakirev provided him with a lot of fervent direction and advice. His catalogue of works is relatively small, perhaps not surprising given that composition was only a sideline to his distinguished scientific career. His greatest musical achievement was the opera *Prince Igor* (based on a medieval Russian epic tale), which combined Russian folksong with an exotic Oriental idiom. However, the most frequently heard today of Borodin's works is his Symphony No. 2 in B minor website 14 . The first movement represents a gathering of Russian knights. Although Borodin makes no use of traditional Russian folk tunes in the work, he treats the arresting and declamatory main theme, heard at the music's very opening, according to the principles of Russian folk music. In the middle section of the movement (2'58"–4'48"),

Alexander Borodin (1833–1887)

he repeats the theme many times fully intact, on different instruments and with different accompaniments – a very similar technique to that used by Glinka in *Kamarinskaya*. A western European composer like Beethoven or Brahms would have taken a very different approach, probably splitting up the main theme into separate motifs and using the fragments to build the musical texture.

Mussorgsky was arguably the greatest of The Five but he also had the shortest life, dying from alcoholism at the age of forty-two. He is best known for his *Pictures at an Exhibition*, a musical representation of an exhibition of works by his artist friend Victor Hartmann, who had recently died. The work was originally written for piano, though it is most often heard today in the orchestral version made by the French composer Maurice Ravel. As with Borodin, Mussorgsky's greatest work was an opera, *Boris Godunov*. Based on events from seventeenth-century Russian history, it masterfully portrays the tensions within the extremely complex Russian class system.

Rimsky-Korsakov was the youngest and most prolific member of The Five. He wrote operas and songs that were closely linked to the Russian folk tradition. Eastern exoticism, similar to that heard in Borodin's *Prince Igor*, is a common element in much of his music, as demonstrated in his best-known work: the orchestral showpiece *Sheherazade*. Towards the end of his life, Rimsky-Korsakov became one of Stravinsky's teachers, and his influence and progressive views helped to shape the innovative harmonic language of Stravinsky's ballet *The Firebird*. In many ways, therefore, Rimsky-Korsakov was more than just a Russian nationalist: he was a gateway to the development of twentieth-century music.

> **"Rimsky was deeply and unshowingly generous,**
> **and unkind only to admirers of Tchaikovsky"**
>
> Igor Stravinsky, *Memories and Commentaries* (1960)

Pyotr Il'yich Tchaikovsky (1840–1893)

Tchaikovsky was born to a middle-class family in Votkinsk, about 500 miles east of Moscow. As Schumann had done thirty years earlier, he embarked on legal studies before changing direction at the age of twenty-three and entering the St Petersburg Conservatory. Here he came into contact with The Five, and initially he was influenced by their nationalist philosophy: his First Symphony 'Winter Daydreams' was a musical depiction of Russian winter scenes, and his Second, the 'Little Russian', was based on Ukrainian folksongs and Russian Orthodox chant.

But as Tchaikovsky matured, music became an outlet for his own emotions, rather than an expression of nationalism. It was a medium through which he could deal with issues that he would not have dared to put into words. He was plagued throughout his life by his inability to come to terms with his homosexuality. The affairs he did have with other men only served to compound the guilt he felt for what he considered his abnormal nature. In a desperate attempt to conform, he married a former student named Antonina Ivanova Miliukova in 1877, pointing out to her that he could never offer her a conventional relationship. Within days of the wedding, he

Pyotr Il'yich Tchaikovsky (1840–1893)

"I love Mozart as a musical Christ"

Pyotr Il'yich Tchaikovsky

realised he had made a terrible mistake. He found Antonina frivolous and irritating, and, although she was well aware of the situation into which she had entered, she took every opportunity to play the role of the exploited and neglected wife as publicly as she could. The emotional turmoil of this episode led Tchaikovsky to attempt suicide by jumping into a river (another incident which calls Schumann's life to mind). He was rescued by his brother Modest, and the only treatment his doctor prescribed for his depression was separation from Antonina (see opposite page).

It was around this time that Tchaikovsky formed an extraordinary relationship with a rich widow called Nadezhda von Meck. She had written to him to say how much she loved his music, and to ask if she could help him in any way. Tchaikovsky replied, boldly suggesting that she fund him completely, on the condition that they never meet. She agreed, and for fourteen years she sent him considerable amounts of money and they enjoyed an intimate and honest correspondence by letter. Only once did they accidentally come face to face in a concert hall: it caused such embarrassment and discomfort to both parties that they immediately hurried away in opposite directions without exchanging a word.

Tchaikovsky dedicated his first truly mature symphony, the Fourth, to Mme von Meck. It opens with the brass playing the famous 'Fate' motif, which returns in the final movement and which Tchaikovsky described as 'a force which, like the sword of Damocles, hangs perpetually over our heads and is always embittering the soul'. Reading these words, it comes as no surprise that this symphony was written around the

Looking back on his disastrous marriage, Tchaikovsky reveals the level of torment it caused him:

I got married in accordance with the dictates, not of the heart, but of some incomprehensible conjunction of circumstances which led me, as though by fate, to choose the most difficult of options. As soon as the ceremony was over, as soon as I found myself alone with my wife and realised that it was now our destiny to live together, inseparable, I suddenly felt that not only did she not inspire in me even simple friendship but that she was utterly detestable, in the fullest sense of the word. It seemed to me that I, or at least the best, perhaps the only good part of me – my musical talent – had perished beyond recall. So far as my future lot was concerned, the picture rose before my eyes of vegetating miserably, of an utterly intolerable, oppressive farce. I fell into deep despair. I began passionately, hungrily to long for death. Death seemed to me the only way out, but I could not contemplate killing myself. I knew that if I made my mind up to commit suicide it would be a mortal blow to my family. Apart from that, my weakness (if it can be called a weakness) is that I love life, I love my work, I love the successes awaiting me in the future. And finally, I have still not said all that I can and want to say before the time comes to depart for eternity.

time of his brief marriage, and the first movement's main theme (which comes after the 'Fate' motif) evokes all the passion and desperation which came close to killing him. Yet, through all his misery, there is a hint of optimism. The final movements of the Fourth and Fifth symphonies have a positive tone, albeit one tainted by the impression that he does not find the idea of a happy ending entirely convincing.

Tchaikovsky also found refuge from all his worries in the world of ballet. As well as his delightful and irresistible ballet scores such as *The Nutcracker*, *The Sleeping Beauty* and *Swan Lake*, there is much ballet and dance music to be found within his symphonies and operas, music which evokes all the glamour of the ballrooms in Imperialist Russia. The second movement of his Symphony No. 6 in B minor 'Pathétique' (website 15) sounds like a waltz – but it has five as opposed to three beats in the bar, demonstrating Tchaikovsky's skill and inventiveness in modifying standard musical forms. The 'Pathétique' was the work that Tchaikovsky loved more than any of his others. It was also his last work. Just nine days after its premiere in St Petersburg, he was dead.

The official reason given for his death was cholera, of which there was an epidemic at the time. However, this has been the source of much debate over the years: cholera was a disease which was almost exclusively confined to the working classes who lived in areas of poor hygiene, so how would the well-to-do Tchaikovsky have contracted it? One of the more convincing alternative theories in recent years is that Tchaikovsky was forced by the Tsar's regime to commit suicide to cover up the scandal of an affair with a high-ranking young man.

*Sketches of bars 88–96 and 152–63 of Tchaikovsky's
Symphony No. 6 'Pathétique', second movement,
in the composer's own hand*

Although Tchaikovsky was an exact contemporary of The Five, he never became part of the group. They regarded his music, which betrayed his love of Mozart and Bizet, as too westernised. As already mentioned, Tchaikovsky's music is more about the composer's psyche than his country. Having said that, it never totally loses sight of the nationalist ideal, and his mature works frequently contain references to folksong: the final movement of the Fourth Symphony is a portrayal of a national festival and is based on the folksong *In the fields there stood a birch*; likewise, folksongs underpin the final movements of two of his most famous works: the Violin Concerto and the Piano Concerto No. 1. (The latter, originally intended for Nikolai Rubinstein, was dedicated to Hans von Bülow, who gave its premiere in Boston. Rubinstein judged it badly composed and unplayable but later rescinded his comments and became a first-rate interpreter of the work.) Tchaikovsky's musical inspiration often drew upon events from his own life. There were the autobiographical elements of the last three symphonies; in addition, Tchaikovsky clearly identified with the subject matter of his greatest and most deeply felt opera, *Eugene Onegin*. Based on Pushkin's story, the opera tells of the devastating effects caused by Onegin's suppression of his feelings for Tatyana, who ends up embarking on a socially appropriate but loveless marriage.

It could be said that Tchaikovsky's music takes a more subtle approach to nationalism than that of other composers. Although primarily about himself, his music is considered today to be profoundly Russian: in this way, the psyche of the individual can be thought to be formed by, and therefore be part of, a national psyche. It is ironic that although Tchaikovsky consciously chose not to bang the nationalist drum as overtly as his colleagues, he did more than any of them to raise the international profile of Russian music.

Bohemia

Bedřich Smetana (1824–1884)

It might seem strange that the composer who is credited with establishing the Czech national music style was a native German speaker and only learned to speak faltering Czech as a mature adult. But Bohemia, as much of today's Czech Republic was called in the nineteenth century, had been under Austrian rule since 1526 and German was the official language of business. As a result, Czech fell out of common usage until the rise of nationalism in the nineteenth century heralded a renewed sense of pride in local languages and traditions.

Smetana's comic opera *The Bartered Bride* is full of happy peasant scenes, and much of the music is based on popular folk dances, such as the furiant and the polka (which was commonly heard in Bohemia, despite its Polish origins). It was, and still is, one of his most frequently performed works, much to the irritation of Smetana himself, who would have preferred to be remembered for a serious, rather than a comic, opera.

Between 1872 and 1879 he wrote six symphonic poems, collectively known as *Má vlast* ('My Homeland'), which formed his greatest testament to the love he held for his native

Bedřich Smetana (1824–1884)

**"Here is a composer with a genuine Czech heart,
an artist by the Grace of God"**

Franz Liszt on Smetana

country. Each depicts an episode from the history and legends of Bohemia, and is strongly Czech in mood. The second of these poems, 'Vltava' <website 16>, follows the course of the eponymous river as it flows through Bohemia, and Smetana provided a detailed programme in the score: at the very opening we join the Vltava River at its source where two brooks join a stream; it runs through forests and meadows (3'12"), before flowing past the scene of a merry village wedding (4'20"); at nightfall, watersprites are seen dancing in the moonlight (6'15"); we return by day to the flow of the river (8'52") which swirls through the St John Rapids (9'53") before flowing proudly in a broad stream towards Prague (11'10"). The opening theme of this work sounds distinctly Bohemian; and although this theme is regarded today by the Czech people as a national folksong, it is probably based on a song Smetana heard when he spent several years in Sweden. It is because Smetana's music innately expresses something of the Bohemian spirit that he is regarded as the founder of the Czech nationalist style.

Antonín Dvořák (1841–1904)

When Smetana was appointed Music Director of the Provisional Theatre in Prague in the mid-1860s, the viola section of the orchestra was led by a young man who would shortly take over the reins as Bohemia's foremost composer, and who would launch Czech musical nationalism onto a truly international platform. Unlike Smetana, who had had a comfortable middle-class upbringing, Antonín Dvořák was of genuine peasant stock. He was born into a family of butchers

Antonín Dvořák (1841–1904)

**"All the calamities and trials of my young life were
sweetened by music – my guardian angel"**

Antonín Dvořák

in a village north of Prague; Czech was his mother tongue and the rhythms and inflections of this language, as well as those of the folk music he heard when growing up, had a profound influence on his music. His pride in his national heritage was strengthened by his need to fight throughout his life against the condescending snobbery of those who assumed he was stupid due to his provincial ways and his lack of proficiency in German.

By the time he was in his teens Dvořák was showing a rare musical talent. Instead of entering the family trade, as had been his father's intention, he headed off to enrol in the organ school in Prague, thanks to financial support provided by his uncle. Over the next ten years his focus on playing gradually gave way to composition, and, ironically, when his uncle was no longer able to support him, the financial straits in which he found himself proved to be the catalyst to his forming an international reputation. In 1874 he submitted his Third Symphony for the Austrian State Stipendium – a scheme which provided support for poor Austrian musicians. Brahms was on the awards committee and was greatly impressed by the work (even though it showed the influence of Wagner, one of the most vocal anti-Brahmsians). So not only did Dvořák secure a grant and a lifelong friendship with Brahms, but his music was also brought by Brahms to the attention of the publisher Fritz Simrock, with whom he would have a long and fruitful collaboration. The relationship between composer and publisher, however, was not without its tensions: Simrock infuriated Dvořák on several occasions when he failed to hide his belief that Bohemia was a provincial and unsophisticated nation that should accept its

A letter written by Dvořák in September 1885 showed that he had no intention of letting his publisher Fritz Simrock get away with expressing his anti-Czech sentiments:

Oh your last letter with its national-political comments was very entertaining. I only regret that you are so badly informed. That is how all our enemies or, more exactly, certain individuals, must write according to the tendency or intentions of this or that political paper. But what have we two to do with politics? Let us be glad that we can dedicate our services to art. And let us hope that nations which possess and represent art will never perish, no matter how small they are. Forgive me, but I only wanted to say to you that an artist has also his country in which he must have firm faith and for which he must have an ardent heart.

subjugated position within the Austrian Empire. The fact that he made large amounts of money out of Dvořák's most blatantly Bohemian music did nothing to moderate his views (see opposite page). The first of Dvořák's works that Simrock published was a set of Slavonic Dances. Some of the dances use authentic folk tunes, while others are just composed in the style of Bohemian folk music. The Slavonic Dance in C major, Op. 46 No. 1 website 17 is based on the furiant, a traditional Bohemian dance characterised by constantly changing rhythms. The sections beginning at 0'00" and 2'09" have three beats in the bar, while the middle section at 1'08" has four beats in the bar. There are also contrasting rhythms within the first and third sections, which start off with three beats in the bar but contain short, two-beat passages at 0'15" and 2'20" respectively. The result is an evocative, energetic piece which, along with the other Slavonic Dances, has enjoyed sustained popularity ever since its composition.

Dvořák's growing reputation led to an invitation from Tchaikovsky to visit Russia, as well as several invitations to England, where he received the same celebrity treatment that Mendelssohn had enjoyed earlier in the century. By this stage he had reached a level of financial security that enabled him to buy a country house in a village outside Prague called Vysoká, where he settled very comfortably with his wife and six children. However, in 1891 he received a letter from an American lady named Jeanette Thurber, asking him to become the Director of the newly founded National Conservatory of Music in New York. America was a relatively young country and she believed that it needed a helping hand in establishing a national music tradition. Dvořák's achievement in raising the international profile of a peripheral nation such as Bohemia made him an obvious choice for the position. Dvořák was reluctant to leave the blissfully happy life he enjoyed (so rare among Romantic composers) at Vysoká, but the financial offer was such that he could not refuse and he ended up spending three years in America. As Mrs Thurber had hoped, he took particular interest in the traditional music of both the black and the native Americans. Some of his most popular music dates from his years in America, such as his Ninth Symphony, entitled 'From the New World', and his Cello Concerto. It can be tempting to look for American influences in Dvořák's music from this time of his life, and it has been suggested that some sections of the 'New World' symphony were inspired by negro spirituals; but in later life Dvořák maintained that all the music he wrote was essentially Bohemian.

Dvořák's music is fundamentally conservative. He did not break new ground in terms of harmony or form, but his music is characterised by simple, exquisite melodies and a profound beauty imbued with an unmistakable sense of the spirit of Bohemia. That spirit can be heard in a distinctly eastern European melancholic yearning (the opening of the third movement of his Symphony No. 8, for example, has a similar wistful nostalgia to the main theme of Smetana's 'Vltava'), in the joyous abandon of the Slavonic Dances, or the bright and innocent melodies of the string quartets. In addition to his substantial orchestral and chamber music output, Dvořák wrote ten operas. He did not have the same innate dramatic instinct as Wagner or Verdi, and these works are not thought to be among his greatest – though one of them, *Rusalka*, is still occasionally programmed today. His failure to write an opera that scored a similar success to Smetana's *The Bartered Bride* was a great source of disappointment to him towards the end of his life and resulted in a period of depression and illness which lasted until his death in 1904.

Moving West…

Musical nationalism in Europe became less prominent the further west you went. England's island status helped it to remain immune from foreign invasion, and as its national identity was not being challenged composers felt no such pressing need to reinforce it through their music. In any case, there was little music of significance being written in England for most of the nineteenth century, and it was not until the 1880s, with the emergence of composers such as **Charles Villiers Stanford** (1852–1924) and **Hubert Parry** (1848–1918), that there was a gradual renaissance of a rich English music tradition. The English flavour of nationalism is evident in the stately quality of music written by these composers, calling to mind the pomp, ceremony and restraint of Victorian England.

Napoleon's various European campaigns inspired no particular pride in the French, and this is reflected by a lack of national identity in French music throughout most of the century. In fact, any national colour in French music of this time tends to be of the Spanish variety, as heard in *Carmen* by **Georges Bizet** (1838–1875). In Spain itself, there was extremely little music of distinction written for the concert

hall until **Isaac Albéniz** (1860–1909) developed a strong
nationalist tradition from the rich Spanish folk music culture.
This was built upon by composers such as **Manuel de Falla**
(1876–1946) and **Joaquín Rodrigo** (1901–1999) in the
twentieth century.

In France, as in England, it was not until the latter part of
the nineteenth century that there was a renaissance in
musical creativity. One of the first composers to make a
substantial contribution to this revitalisation was **Camille
Saint-Saëns** (1835–1921). He was conscious that the
development of French music was being hindered by the
national fixation on operatic spectaculars, heroic in subject
matter but superficial in substance. Although Saint-Saëns
wrote twelve operas himself, they comprised only a modest
portion of his sizeable catalogue of over 300 works. He
played a pivotal role in effecting a much-needed shift in
French music towards instrumental writing, and, in 1871, he
co-founded the Société National de Musique to encourage
the development of French orchestral and chamber music.
He is best remembered today for three works: the opera
Samson et Dalila, the Symphony No. 3 'Organ' and *The
Carnival of the Animals*. For Saint-Saëns, elegance of melody
and beauty of harmony were of more importance than
emotional depth. Although this has been the source of some
criticism of his work, it is an aesthetic principle which proved
to be a great influence on French composers of the late
nineteenth and early twentieth centuries.

Gabriel Fauré (1845–1924) was a pupil and later a close
friend of Saint-Saëns. He, too, moved away from the French
tradition of writing monumental works on themes of

Gabriel Fauré (1845–1924)

**"For me... music exists to elevate us as far as
possible above everyday existence"**

Gabriel Fauré

revolution and heroism: he was by nature a miniaturist and preferred to write more intimate chamber works with an elegance and harmonic lushness inherited from his teacher. Although it is his Requiem for choir and orchestra for which he is best known, most of his works are much smaller in scale; his many songs are regarded as amongst the greatest in the French repertoire, and he wrote a substantial amount of beautiful, poetic works for solo instruments – such as the Romance in B flat for violin and piano (website 18). From 1896 he was Professor of Composition at the Paris Conservatoire, and his pupils included **Maurice Ravel** (1875–1937) and the great composition teacher **Nadia Boulanger** (1887–1979); thus – finally – a new and specifically French musical tradition began to flourish.

Moving to northern Europe, we once again find a strong nationalist tendency in the music of Scandinavia, of which **Edvard Grieg** (1843–1907) was the greatest exponent. His works were strongly influenced by the melodies and dance rhythms of Norwegian folk music, which appear often in his ten sets of short Lyric Pieces for solo piano, and in his 140 songs, many of which were inspired by his wife, a singer. Greig felt most comfortable working in smaller-scale forms, and yet it is a large-scale work for which he is best known: the harmonically adventurous Piano Concerto in A minor (whose finale is based on a Norwegian dance called the halling). He also wrote a substantial amount of incidental music for the theatre, most notably for *Peer Gynt* by the great Norwegian playwright Henrik Ibsen. Grieg made two orchestral suites from his music to *Peer Gynt*, the

Edvard Grieg (1843–1907)

"I am sure my music has a taste of codfish in it"

Edvard Grieg

first of which regularly features on concert programmes today. The final number of this suite, 'In the Hall of the Mountain King' (website 19), eloquently depicts the unmistakably Norwegian land of the trolls, who are attempting to capture Peer Gynt and turn him into one of them.

Elsewhere in Scandinavia, the Finnish composer **Jean Sibelius** (1865–1957) and the Dane **Carl Nielsen** (1865–1931) were the other great nationalist composers of the time. Nielsen's music often stemmed from the experiences of his impoverished but happy childhood. He wrote many songs for which he drew upon the traditional Danish folksongs that his mother often sang to him when he was a boy; and his cantata *Springtime on Funen* (1921) is a nostalgic depiction of the beautiful island where he spent his youth.

Sibelius grew up at a time when nationalist feelings were running strong among the Finns as a consequence of the Russian domination of their country. His early works were often inspired by nationalist themes, such as *Kullervo* (written in 1892 and based on the Finnish national epic, the *Kalevala*) and *Finlandia*, which became something of a second Finnish national anthem following its premiere in 1899.

Nielsen and Sibelius both defined a new musical language for their countries, but their nationalist idioms were of a progressive nature (most evident in their important and innovative symphonic cycles) and, despite having roots in Romantic expression, they belong essentially to the modern era. The composers each established a strong national tradition in musical creativity, and this continues to flourish today: a large number of the most highly regarded contemporary composers of our time come from Denmark and Finland.

VII. The Epic Austrian Symphonists

Anton Bruckner (1824–1896)

"Bruckner! He is my man!"

Richard Wagner

Anton Bruckner (1824–1896)

Although Bruckner is best known for his nine symphonies, he in fact wrote eleven. Of the two 'extra' symphonies, he regarded one as just an exercise, and he named the other Symphony No. 0, adding a typically humble and self-deprecating remark to the score: 'Only an attempt – totally worthless'. He expanded symphonic form further than any previous composer; his symphonies are characterised by their vast scale (his Eighth lasts around one hour and forty minutes) and by the way in which they move in massive blocks of orchestral sound, as if he were pulling out different organ stops for each section of music.

The analogy of his style to that of organ music is a significant one, as this instrument was an important feature throughout his life. From the age of ten, Bruckner regularly deputised for his father as church organist in the Austrian village of Ansfelden, and when he became a chorister at the nearby monastery school of St Florian he spent much of his time there at the organ. After teaching for fifteen years he was appointed organist of Linz Cathedral at the age of thirty-two. It was another ten years before he really started composing in earnest, by which time his thinking was permeated by organ music to such an extent that his own style could hardly avoid its influence. In 1868 he combined his teaching skills and professional musicianship when he became a lecturer at the Vienna Conservatory.

Bruckner himself was a curious character. Socially introverted and endearingly self-effacing, he lacked the larger-than-life ego typical of most Romantic composers. He longed for a wife but consistently fell for women who were far too young for him. The nearest he came to marriage was just five years before his death, when he fell in love with a hotel chambermaid who was a third of his age. Eventually he abandoned the idea when she declared herself unwilling to convert from the Lutheran to the Roman Catholic Church. His religion was deeply important to him, and other than his symphonies (the Ninth, incomplete when he died, was dedicated to God himself) his most significant pieces were liturgical choral works. He was prone to bouts of depression and nervous instability: he was committed to a sanatorium for three months in his thirties, where he developed numeromania – a condition which led him to count obsessively, whether it be blades of grass, grains of sand or simply bars of music, each of which he would number individually in the scores of his symphonies.

Bruckner's musical hero was Wagner: he dedicated his Third Symphony to him, and the finale of his most accessible symphony, the Seventh, was inspired by Wagner's death. Wagner, in turn, seems to have reciprocated his admiration and the two composers became friends, although the word 'friendship' doesn't seem quite appropriate given Bruckner's almost embarrassing obsequiousness when talking to Wagner: once, when Wagner asked him if he had heard *Parsifal*, Bruckner's response was to kneel down, kiss Wagner's hand, and say, 'Oh master, I worship you!'

Bruckner's association with Wagner made him an unpopular figure in some camps. The highly influential critic Eduard Hanslick, who loathed everything Wagner stood for, predictably wrote damning reviews of all Bruckner's works, precipitating many of the composer's depressive phases.

However, despite the fact that Bruckner and Wagner were closely associated in the minds of the Viennese public, they were essentially quite different composers. There are superficial similarities between their works in terms of sheer length, and the long-flowing melodic lines that were characteristic of both composers; but there are more significant fundamental differences: Bruckner's harmonies and modest orchestration seem to follow on from earlier composers such as Schubert, rather than emulating the radical and progressive example of Wagner. Moreover, Bruckner's works are conceived in separate blocks or sections (suggesting the influence of organ music as mentioned above) rather than in a seamless Wagnerian style.

Gustav Mahler (1860–1911)

As with Bruckner, Mahler's compositional output is dominated by his series of nine epic symphonies. They contain an intensity of personal expression that stretched the Romantic idiom to its limits: his music is often thought of as a bridge leading from the Romantic era to the twentieth century. It is as intrinsically autobiographical as Tchaikovsky's music, embodying the many complex and contrasting facets of Mahler's charismatic personality.

Like so many Romantic artists, Mahler felt most at home in the countryside. Despite suffering from an involuntary tic in his leg he loved walking and mountain-climbing, and there are many moments in his works when the listener feels transported to the Austrian Alps – halfway through the first movement of his Sixth Symphony, for example, when he uses

Gustav Mahler (1860–1911)

**"To write a symphony is,
for me, to construct the world"**

Gustav Mahler

cowbells, or in the third movement of the Fifth with the sound of the horns calling to each other across a valley. But Mahler's world was not simply one of unadulterated idyll. His music also portrayed the dark side of his character, caused in part by the difficult experiences of his childhood: the endemic anti-Semitism in Austria in the late nineteenth century, the death of six brothers and sisters, and his parents' constant fighting all took their toll on Mahler's view of the world. The combination of an inherent optimism and bitter experience often comes out in his music, when a light-hearted passage is distorted into something almost grotesque. Mahler himself thought that this combination of innocence and bitter irony could be traced back to an event he remembered from his childhood: to escape a fierce argument between his parents, he ran out of the house onto the street and came across a hurdy-gurdy playing the popular Viennese air *Ach du lieber Augustin*.

The duality can be heard in the haunting third movement of his Symphony No. 1 'Titan' website 20 . It is based on the well-known French tune *Frère Jacques*, normally a jolly and carefree children's song, but Mahler puts it in the minor key and turns it into a funeral march. In the two-minute section beginning at 2'10", another tune is heard fluctuating between major and minor keys, making it impossible to determine whether the music is happy or sad. There are moments when the orchestra sounds like a military band (e.g. at 3'16" and 8'01"): this is a characteristic Mahlerian sound, stemming from his childhood love of hearing military bands march through his home town. Another idiosyncratic orchestral sound is heard at 8'21", when the very shrill-sounding clarinets almost bring the music into the realm of the grotesque.

In addition to his composing, Mahler also had an extremely demanding career as an opera conductor. After Mahler had graduated from the Vienna Conservatory (where he had become friends with Bruckner, a lecturer there) he began conducting musical comedies in the health resort of Hall in Upper Austria, purely as a way of staving off poverty. But he had a real talent, and he found that conducting gave him the outward physical exercise he needed to counterbalance the creative activity that was always going on inside his head. He received successive appointments to increasingly high-profile opera houses, such as Leipzig, Budapest, Hamburg and Vienna (where he had to convert from Judaism to Roman Catholicism in order to be considered for the post). His favourite operas were those by Wagner, and his unwavering veneration of the great man makes one wonder what he thought of Wagner's anti-Semitic tendencies. Mahler's conducting responsibilities therefore largely restricted his composition to the summer months, when he would retire to a lakeside village, finding inspiration in the natural surroundings.

In 1901 he fell deeply in love with, and married, Alma Schindler, a *femme fatale* nineteen years his junior whose previous lovers included the artists Klimt and Zemlinsky. It was not an easy relationship. Alma was self-centred and, by her own admission, incapable of emotional warmth. But being married to a genius such as Mahler was no easy ride: he was a perfectionist for whom music came before everything else. He also actively discouraged Alma's considerable talent for composition (just as Schumann had suppressed Clara's, sixty years earlier). Shortly before his death he revised his stance and started encouraging her to compose, even arranging for some of her songs to be published.

Despite their differences there was a strong bond between them. In Alma, Mahler had found his muse, and his rate of composition accelerated considerably after he met her: in the preceding twenty years he had only written four symphonies and some songs, but in the final decade remaining to him he wrote five more huge symphonies, the so-called 'song-symphony' *Das Lied von der Erde* ('The Song of the Earth') and the song cycle *Kindertotenlieder* ('Songs on the Death of Children'). Despite its seemingly depressing title, *Kindertotenlieder* is a transcendent, spiritually uplifting work that typifies Mahler's ability to overcome adversity. In fact, it was tragically prophetic of his elder daughter's death two years after its composition. His symphonies do contain much music that is dark and foreboding, yet, with the exception of the Sixth, they all end in major keys.

In 1907 Mahler received his last appointment, as conductor of New York's Metropolitan Opera. For the next three-and-a-half years he and Alma divided their time between Austria and America. These years were marred both by politics in the opera house and by the diagnosis of a serious heart condition. He died in 1911 from a resulting blood infection. Alma survived him by fifty-three years.

VIII. The End of Romanticism

Richard Strauss (1864–1949)

"I employ cacophony to outrage people"

Richard Strauss

It is difficult to pinpoint a specific time when Romanticism in music ended and so-called modern music began (the term 'modern music' is still used today to refer to music written a century ago). After Beethoven, composers had liberally adapted the rules of harmony and form to their own needs until, by the end of the nineteenth century, there were scarcely any rules left at all: Romanticism had become an umbrella term for many diverse strands of style and genre, each of which progressed towards the new era at its own pace.

Two of the key musical trends which developed throughout the nineteenth century were an increasingly daring and advanced harmonic language, and an increasingly intense and often passionate mode of expression. It was inevitable that there would come a point at which tonal harmony and personal expression could go no further. Clearly, Wagner's 'Tristan' chord, with its indefinable harmonic implications, is an important landmark in the move away from tonality, and Wagner's complex harmonies were a profound influence on the French composer **Claude Debussy** (1862–1918), one of the first composers to leave Romanticism behind him. Debussy's sophisticated chromatic harmonies follow on directly from those of *Tristan*, and his work *Prélude à l'après-midi d'un faune*, written between 1892 and 1894, has been dubbed the 'first piece of modern music'. Debussy was interested in how specific chords could contribute to the overall orchestral sound, rather than whether they made harmonic sense. For him, colour was infinitely more important than key. Debussy is known as an 'impressionist' composer, as his colourful, lush and blurred sonorities can be seen as the musical equivalent of paintings by Monet, Manet and Renoir. He initiated a much-needed revival in the French music tradition, after its fairly undistinguished track record through the nineteenth century.

Other composers took different routes into the realms of modernism. **Arnold Schoenberg** (1874–1951) was born in Austria and studied with Mahler. His early compositions, which include some delightful songs as well as the beautiful string work *Verklärte Nacht* ('Transfigured Night'), conform very much to the Romantic idiom. However, in the early 1920s he abandoned tonality – and Romanticism – by developing a radical system of absolute atonality known as 'serial' or 'twelve-note' music, in which each of the twelve semitones in the western scale was given equal importance.

While some composers abandoned the traditions of the past in order to invent a new language for the modern era, there were others who maintained the Romantic idiom well into the twentieth century.

Richard Strauss (1864–1949)

For the first half of his life, the German composer Richard Strauss (not related to the famous composer of waltzes, Johann Strauss) was a provocative and radical figure. He inherited the tradition of the symphonic poem from Liszt, and in the last decade of the nineteenth century he wrote eight of his ten tone poems (as he preferred to call them), the best known of which are *Don Juan*, *Till Eulenspiegel* and *Also sprach Zarathustra*. In some respects they are conventional works: Strauss, as well as employing a well-established genre, used in them some distinctly un-modern techniques, such as fugue, sonata form, and theme and variations. Yet in other respects they break new ground, containing an overtly heightened emotional power that is better described as 'decadent' than 'Romantic'. In 1900 he turned his attention towards the stage and took the world by storm with his first major opera: *Salome* (1904), based on Oscar Wilde's play. Much of the music in *Salome* is lush and Romantic, but it moves through the decadent language of the tone poems, becoming more distorted, almost depraved, until Salome, on seeing the severed head of John the Baptist, reaches a frenzy of erotic excitement. This artistic style, in which extreme emotion becomes so overindulged that pleasure and aesthetic beauty give way to grotesqueness, is known as 'expressionism'. Expressionism was an artistic movement that was seen in all art forms, the most famous Expressionist work being Edvard Munch's painting *The Scream*.

In around 1910 Strauss reverted to a much more conservative style, and most of his music written after this time looked back to the heritage of the previous century: his tone poem *An Alpine Symphony*, written between 1911 and 1915, is an entirely Romantic work, containing beautiful musical depictions of Alpine scenes and contrasting strongly with the avant-garde works with which his colleagues shocked their audiences (Stravinsky's arch-modern ballet *The Rite of Spring* caused a riot at its premiere in 1913); his comic opera *Der Rosenkavalier* (1911) looks back to the idiom of Verdi's *Falstaff* or Wagner's *Die Meistersinger von Nürnberg*; and his last and best-known work, the *Four Last*

Songs, written in 1948, has a tender passion which proves that Strauss always kept one foot firmly in the world of Romanticism.

Giacomo Puccini (1858–1924)

Puccini's operas represent the pinnacle of pure Romantic expression. Following on from Verdi's tradition, he was drawn towards melodramatic plots which generally ended up with the tragic death of the heroine. He scored his first success in 1896 with *La Bohème*, which despite an extremely simple plot is filled with such ravishing melodies and harmonies, and is so well paced dramatically, that it has riveted audiences for over a century. He followed *La Bohème* with two more operas which quickly became staple operatic repertoire: *Tosca*, based on Victorien Sardou's violent play set during the Napoleonic wars in Rome at the beginning of the nineteenth century, and *Madama Butterfly*, in which he demonstrated his powerful gift for orchestration by the subtle juxtaposition of Japanese and western sounds. Orientalism was very fashionable at the end of the nineteenth and the beginning of the twentieth centuries (it had featured in many works by the Russian Five) and Puccini returned to this style for his final work *Turandot* (left incomplete at the composer's death), in which the cruel Chinese Princess Turandot offers her hand to the suitor who can answer her three riddles correctly, and beheads those who cannot.

Puccini's music is unashamedly accessible, and throughout his entire career he consistently produced unforgettable tunes such as 'Che gelida manina' from *La*

Giacomo Puccini (1858–1924)

"Puccini looks to me more like the heir of Verdi than any of his rivals"

George Bernard Shaw, after the London premiere of *Manon Lescaut*

Bohème, 'Vissi d'arte' from *Tosca*, 'O mio babbino caro' from *Gianni Schicchi*, and most famously 'Nessun Dorma' from *Turandot*. Many of the more cutting-edge composers of the day, whose radical new works were challenging contemporary audiences, frowned upon the accessibility of Puccini's music. Yet, his unsurpassed ability to create realistic characters, to build up dramatic tension, and to tug at the heartstrings of his audience without resorting to cliché (one thinks of the death of Mimì at the end of *La Bohème*, or the torture scene from Act II of *Tosca*) has ensured that he is one of the most regularly performed opera composers today.

Sergei Rachmaninov (1873–1943)

Following in the Romantic tradition of virtuoso composer–pianists, Rachmaninov was the greatest exponent of this phenomenon in the twentieth century, as Liszt had been in the nineteenth. He had a delicate temperament which plagued him sporadically throughout his life, mostly notably when he was in his mid-twenties. In 1897 the premiere of his First Symphony was a critical disaster (due less to the quality of the music than to the fact that the conductor, composer Alexander Glazunov, was drunk for the performance). Rachmaninov fell into a deep depression that led to a three-year period of writer's block, which he eventually overcame with the help of hypnotherapy. The unleashing of his blocked creative powers resulted in the Piano Concerto No. 2, which has become one of the most popular pieces of classical music ever written – a reputation which was only enhanced by its use in the 1945 film *Brief*

Sergei Rachmaninov (1873–1943)

"How can I compose without melody?"

Sergei Rachmaninov

Encounter. The following sixteen years were the most prolific of his career: he produced solo piano works, songs, two operas, choral works, his Second Symphony and his Third Piano Concerto (which recently experienced a surge in popularity through its use in another high-profile film, *Shine*, which told the story of the mentally disturbed Australian pianist David Helfgott).

Following the Bolshevik Revolution of 1917, Rachmaninov fled Russia with his family for the USA. There followed another period of creative silence, lasting nine years, during which time he dedicated his energies to piano playing. He began to compose again in 1926, writing his Fourth Piano Concerto (he gave the premiere himself in Philadelphia). In the remaining seventeen years of his life, he only wrote another five works.

Rachmaninov was the last great Russian Romantic composer. By the time the next generation came along, which included Stravinsky (born in 1882, just nine years after Rachmaninov) and Prokofiev (born in 1891), modernism had taken hold of Europe, and composers adopted a harsher, less emotionally indulgent style. Rachmaninov's musical language, with its broad sweeping phrases tainted by melancholy, descended directly from the distinctly Russian Romantic sound of Tchaikovsky. The brooding eastern European melancholy can be heard in his Prelude in C sharp minor, Op. 3 No. 2 (website 21), which was written in 1892, and was his most popular recital piece (although Rachmaninov was asked so often to include it in his own recitals that he ended up hating it).

Sir Edward Elgar (1857–1934)

In any overview of nineteenth-century music, England is conspicuous for its low profile. In fact, there were extremely few significant British composers from the end of the seventeenth century (after the death of Purcell) until the beginning of the twentieth. Sir Arthur Sullivan (1842–1900) is the only figure to have become a household name in this period, through the comic operas he wrote with the librettist W.S. Gilbert. As explained earlier, Stanford and Parry initiated something of an English nationalist style, but it was not until Elgar arrived on the scene that a British musical tradition of international importance re-emerged.

Elgar was largely self-taught as a musician. His father owned a music shop in Worcester, so he used the opportunity to teach himself a number of different instruments, and he learnt the art of composition not by attending a prestigious London music college but by writing pieces for local amateur music organisations. It took a long time for Elgar to build a reputation. Following his marriage to a general's daughter in 1889, he moved to London in an attempt to break into the musical establishment there. The attempt failed and the couple ended up moving back to Malvern.

It was in 1899 that his most famous work, the 'Enigma' Variations (the 'Enigma' refers to the still unidentified tune on which the main theme is based), brought Elgar to both national and international attention. Each variation is a musical portrait of one of his friends (except the final variation, which depicts himself). The most famous of these is 'Nimrod' website 22 , portraying August Jaeger, who worked for Elgar's publisher Novello (see page 130). The wistful melody

Sir Edward Elgar (1857–1934)

*"...there is music in the air, music all
around us, the world is full of it and you
simply take as much as you require"*

Sir Edward Elgar

and predominance of the strings in the orchestra is typically Elgarian, showing the influence of Brahms yet evoking the stately and noble quality of Edwardian England: it is this sound which has led Elgar's music to be referred to as 'quintessentially English'.

The following year saw the premiere of Elgar's great oratorio *The Dream of Gerontius*, whereupon Richard Strauss hailed him as the 'first progressive English musician'. Further accolades came when Hans Richter in 1908 conducted the premiere of the first of Elgar's two symphonies, describing it as 'the greatest symphony of modern times, by the greatest modern composer'. In 1920, the year after Elgar composed his Cello Concerto, Lady Elgar died, taking with her much of her husband's creative inspiration. He wrote few works of major significance after his bereavement.

Elgar, as Hans Richter intimated, is a composer who belongs to the twentieth century. Yet his music never lost track of its roots, which lay in a Romantic mode of expression. He re-established a British music tradition which was to be built upon by the following generation of composers, including Ralph Vaughan Williams, Gustav Holst and Benjamin Britten, and which still profoundly influences many British composers working today.

Into a New Age...

The Romantic era drew to a close in many ways, at many times, and for many reasons. In musical terms, it was not simply the case that the Romantic style had run its course, forcing composers in the twentieth century to find a new

In 1898, when he had first sketched out the 'Enigma' Variations, Elgar wrote to August Jaeger at his publishers Novello about the new work:

...since I've been back I have sketched a set of Variations (orkestra) on an original theme: the variations have amused me because I've labelled 'em with the nicknames of my particular friends – you are Nimrod. That is to say I've written the variations each one to respond to the mood of the 'party'. I've liked to imagine the 'party' writing the var: him (or her) self and have written what I think they wd. have written – if they were asses enough to compose – its a quaint idea & the result is amusing to those behind the scenes & won't affect the hearer who 'nose nuffin'. What think you?

Much love and sunshine,
Ed. Elgar

idiom for the modern age: there were broader issues which changed the cultural climate of the world. Great music has always captured the Zeitgeist, or the spirit of the age, and this was no exception at the outset of the twentieth century, when many countries entered politically turbulent times that were darker and fuelled by less optimism than the revolutions of the previous century. As Napoleon's lofty ideals had once been warped by his ambition, so did the nationalist movement, which had started out with the aim of empowering the common man, become distorted in some countries, leading to violent and repressive regimes at both extremes of the political spectrum. In Germany, the glorification of the national spirit led to a belief in racial superiority, feeding in turn the growing anti-Semitism (rife throughout Europe) and culminating horrifically in the Holocaust. Perhaps the violent decadence of some of Richard Strauss's music reflected this national mood. (It should be said that Strauss himself had a good number of Jewish friends, although he was unjustly accused of being a Nazi collaborator.) In Russia, the overthrowing of the Tsarist dynasty resulted not in a country where all citizens enjoyed a life of plenty, but in decades of brutal dictatorship; composers of the Soviet era, such as Shostakovich and Prokofiev, were not able to convey their experience through a lush Romantic idiom: much of their music is harsh, and menacingly powerful.

Yet, if we jump forward to the present day, we find that there is still a lot of music being written – whether it be an orchestral work by a cutting-edge composer, or a commercial Hollywood film score – which contains lavish harmonies and sweeping melodies inherited from the language of the Romantic composers. In a wider sense, the quest of the individual today for personal expression, self-fulfilment and equal rights for all members of our society is not so far removed from the aims of the Romantic revolutionaries 200 years ago. So perhaps, in spite of the events of the twentieth century that changed the world beyond recognition, the powerful message of the Romantic spirit has never really left us.

Sources of Featured Panels

Pages 22–3: Siepmann, Jeremy, *Beethoven: Life and Works*, Naxos, 2001

Page 35:   Siepmann, Jeremy, *Liszt: Life and Works*, Naxos, 2001

Page 50:   Todd, R. Larry, *Mendelssohn: The Hebrides and other overtures*, Cambridge University Press, 1993

Page 59:   Siepmann, Jeremy, *Brahms: Life and Works*, Naxos, 2002

Page 70:   Siepmann, Jeremy, *Verdi: Life and Works*, Naxos, 2003

Page 81:   Taylor, Ronald, *Richard Wagner: His Life and Times*, Paul Elek Ltd, 1979

Page 91:   Siepmann, Jeremy, *Tchaikovsky: Life and Works*, Naxos, 2002

Page 100:   Siepmann, Jeremy, *Dvořák: Life and Works*, Naxos, 2004

A Timeline of the Romantic Era

	Music	History
1789		beginning of French Revolution
1790		
1791	Mozart dies; Haydn's first visit to England	
1792	Rossini born	French republic declared
1793		Louis XVI and Marie Antoinette executed in Paris
1794		
1795	Haydn completes twelve 'London' symphonies	
1796		
1797	Schubert born; Donizetti born	

Art and Architecture	Literature
	Blake *Songs of Innocence*
éricault born	Thomas Paine *The Rights of Man*
r Joshua Reynolds dies	Shelley born; Mary Wollstonecraft *A Vindication of the Rights of Women*
avid *The Death of Marat*; Brandenburg ate, Berlin	J.P.F. Richter ('Jean Paul') *The Invisible Lodge*
	Blake *Songs of Experience*
	Keats born
orot born	Goethe *Wilhelm Meisters Lehrjahre*
	Coleridge *Kubla Khan*

	Music	History
1798	Haydn *The Creation*	
1799		Napoleon appointed First Consul in France
1800	Beethoven Symphony No. 1	
1801	Bellini born	
1802		
1803	Berlioz born; Beethoven Symphony No. 3 'Eroica'	France sells Louisiana to USA; John Dalton proposes atomic theory
1804		Napoleon crowned Emperor
1805	Beethoven *Fidelio*	Nelson dies at Battle of Trafalgar
1806		
1807		
1808	Beethoven Symphony No. 6 'Pastoral'	Napoleon's troops occupy Spain
1809	Mendelssohn born; Haydn dies; Beethoven Piano Concerto No. 5 'Emperor'	

Art and Architecture	Literature
lacroix born	Coleridge and Wordsworth *Lyrical Ballads*
	Hölderlin *Hyperion*; Schiller *Wallenstein*
oya *Family of Charles IV*	
	Madame de Staël *Delphine*
	Schiller *William Tell*
David *The Coronation of Napoleon*	Wordsworth *Poems in Two Volumes*
Caspar David Friedrich *The Cross in the Mountains*; Blake *The Last Judgement*	Goethe *Faust* (part 1)
	Tennyson born

	Music	History
1810	Chopin born; Schumann born; Paganini makes first tour of Europe	
1811	Liszt born	
1812		Napoleon's disastrous retreat from Moscow
1813	Wagner born; Verdi born	Austria and Prussia declare war on France; Mexico declares independence from Spain
1814		allied forces enter Paris; Napoleon abdicates
1815		Napoleon returns from exile, defeated at Waterloo
1816	Rossini *The Barber of Seville*	
1817		
1818		Spain cedes Florida to USA
1819		
1820		

Art and Architecture	Literature
...unge *Morning*; Goya begins series of ...chings *The Disasters of War*	
	Charles Dickens born; Byron *Childe Harold's Pilgrimage* (first part)
	Jane Austen *Pride and Prejudice*
...illet born; Ingres *Grande Odalisque*	Rückert *Poems*; Scott *Waverley*
...urner *The Founding of Carthage*	
	E.T.A. Hoffmann *The Devil's Elixir*
	Jane Austen dies
	Mary Shelley *Frankenstein*
...ourbet born; Ruskin born; Géricault *The Raft of the Medusa*	Schopenhauer *The World as Will and Idea*; Byron *Don Juan* (first part); Scott *Ivanhoe*
...Brighton Pavilion completed (John Nash)	Pushkin *Ruslan and Ludmila*; Shelley *Prometheus Unbound*; Keats *The Eve of St Agnes and other poems*

	Music	History
1821	Weber *Der Freischütz*	War of Greek independence against Turkey; Michael Faraday discovers electromagnetic induction
1822	Beethoven last piano sonatas; Schubert 'Unfinished' Symphony	Liberia founded as colony for freed US slaves
1823	Schubert *Die schöne Müllerin*	
1824	Bruckner born; Smetana born; Beethoven Ninth Symphony	
1825		trades unions legalised in Britain; firs passenger railway Stockton–Darlingto
1826	Beethoven last string quartets; Weber *Oberon*	
1827	Beethoven dies; Schubert *Winterreise*	Turkish fleet destroyed by French, Russian and British fleets at Navarino
1828	Schubert dies	blast furnace invented
1829	Rossini *William Tell*; Mendelssohn tours Britain	Joseph Henry designs an electric motor; William Burt patents first typewriter in America
1830	Berlioz *Symphonie fantastique*; Mendelssohn *The Hebrides*	Revolution in Paris, Louis Philippe becomes 'citizen king'; Greece proclaimed as independent kingdom; Liverpool and Manchester Railway opens

Art and Architecture	Literature
Constable *The Haywain*	Dostoevsky born; Keats dies; Heine *Poems*; Shelley *Defence of Poetry*
	Shelley dies; E.T.A. Hoffmann dies
Géricault dies; National Gallery in London founded	Byron dies; Pushkin *Boris Godunov*
David dies; Blake *Book of Job* engravings	
Blake dies; Delacroix *The Death of Sardanapalus*	
Goya dies	Ibsen born; Tolstoy born; Pushkin *Eugene Onegin*
	Stendhal *The Red and the Black*

	Music	History
1831	Bellini *Norma*	Faraday constructs a dynamo
1832		Reform Act enlarges parliamentary franchise in Britain
1833	Brahms born	
1834	Berlioz *Harold in Italy*	slavery abolished in the British Empire
1835	Bellini dies; Donizetti *Lucia di Lammermoor*	
1836	Liszt *Album d'un voyageur;* Chopin meets George Sand	Charles Darwin returns from voyage on *HMS Beagle*
1837	Berlioz Requiem	Victoria becomes Queen of England; Frobel opens the first kindergarten
1838	Liszt *Transcendental Studies after Paganini*	beginning of Chartist movement, campaigning for voting rights
1839	Mussorgsky born; Chopin 24 Preludes	developmeny of first reliable way of taking photographs
1840	Tchaikovsky born; Schumann *Dichterliebe*	penny post instituted in Britain
1841	Chabrier born; Wagner *The Flying Dutchman*	
1842	Glinka *Ruslan and Ludmila*	ether first used as anaesthetic

Art and Architecture	Literature
elacroix *Liberty Leading the People*	Hugo *The Hunchback of Notre-Dame*
anet born	Goethe dies; Walter Scott dies
	Tennyson *Poems*
lliam Morris born	Balzac *Le Père Goriot*
	Büchner *Danton's Death*
uses of Parliament, London (Charles rry)	Dickens *The Pickwick Papers*
nstable dies; Delacroix *Women of ziers*	
ner *The Fighting Téméraire*	Dickens *Oliver Twist*
zanne born; Sisley born	Lermontov *A Hero of Our Time*
par David Friedrich dies; Monet born	Zola born; Poe *Tales of the Grotesque*
noir born	
	Mallarmé born; Gogol *Dead Souls*; Macaulay *Lays of Ancient Rome*

	Music	History
1843	Grieg born	
1844	Rimsky-Korsakov born; Mendelssohn Violin Concerto	
1845	Fauré born; Schumann Piano Concerto; Wagner *Tannhäuser*	beginning of Irish potato famine
1846	Berlioz *La Damnation de Faust*; Mendelssohn *Elijah*	sewing machine invented
1847	Mendelssohn dies	
1848	Donizetti dies; Wagner *Lohengrin*	revolutions throughout Europe; publication of *Communist Manifesto* in Paris Louis Philippe abdicates, Louis Napoleon elected president
1849	Chopin dies	
1850		German Confederation restored under Austrian leadership; Public Libraries Act (Britain)
1851	Verdi *Rigoletto*	Great Exhibition in London
1852		Second Empire begins in France, Louis Napoleon now Emperor Napoleon III

Art and Architecture	Literature
skin *Modern Painters*, Vol. 1	
ner *Rain, Steam, and Speed*	Verlaine born; Dumas *The Three Musketeers*
	Charlotte Brontë *Jane Eyre*; Emily Brontë *Wuthering Heights*
uguin born; Pre-Raphaelite therhood founded	
el de Ville completed, Paris (Godde Lesueur)	Dickens *David Copperfield*
irbet shows three paintings at Paris n	Wordsworth dies; Balzac dies; Maupassant born; Tennyson *In Memoriam*; Public Libraries Act (Britain)
stal Palace built to house Great bition, London (Joseph Paxton)	Melville *Moby-Dick*
e Montparnasse, Paris (Lenoir)	Dickens *Bleak House*

	Music	History
1853	Verdi *La traviata*; Wagner begins to write music for *Das Rheingold*	Crimean War begins (Britain, Franc and Turkey vs Russia)
1854	Liszt *Les Préludes*	
1855		
1856	Schumann dies	
1857	Wagner begins work on *Tristan and Isolde*	
1858	Puccini born; Offenbach *Orpheus in the Underworld*	
1859	Gounod *Faust*	Darwin publishes *On the Origin c Species by Means of Natural Selection*
1860	Mahler born	first Italian parliament held at Turi Garibaldi conquers Naples and Si
1861		Italy united as one kingdom; American Civil War begins
1862	Debussy born	
1863	Berlioz *The Trojans*; Bizet *The Pearl Fishers*	

Art and Architecture	Literature
an Gogh born; Haussmann begins shaping centre of Paris	
addington station, London (Brunel)	Thoreau *Walden*
niversal Exhibition, Paris offers etrospectives of Ingres and Delacroix	
	Flaubert *Madame Bovary*
Aillet *The Gleaners*; Museum of Ornamental Art (later V & A) founded, ondon	Baudelaire *Les Fleurs du mal*
Aillet *The Angelus*	Dickens *A Tale of Two Cities*
	Chekhov born
Gare du Nord, Paris (Hittorff)	
	Hugo *Les Misérables*
Delacroix dies; Manet *Le Déjeuner sur l'herbe*	

	Music	History
1864	Richard Strauss born	Prussia and Austria take Schleswig-Holstein from Denmark
1865	Sibelius born; Wagner *Tristan and Isolde*	
1866	Offenbach *La Vie parisienne*	transatlantic telegraph cable laid by Brunel's *Great Eastern*
1867		Prussians head new North German Confederation; kingdom of Austria-Hungary founded
1868		
1869	Berlioz dies	Suez Canal opens; women granted votes in US state of Wyoming
1870		Franco-Prussian War; Napoleon III surrenders at Sedan, Paris besieged
1871		Paris Commune followed by repression; armistice with Prussia; Rome becomes capital of Italy
1872	Mussorgsky *Boris Godunov*	
1873	Rachmaninov born	

Art and Architecture	Literature
anet *Olympia*	Carroll *Alice's Adventures in Wonderland*
	Dostoevsky *Crime and Punishment*
gres dies	Baudelaire dies; Ibsen *Peer Gynt*; Marx *Kapital* (part 1)
	Browning *The Ring and the Book*; Alcott *Little Women*
Matisse born	Tolstoy *War and Peace*
	Proust born
Monet *Impression, Sunrise*	George Eliot *Middlemarch*
	Tolstoy *Anna Karenina*; Rimbaud *Une Saison en enfer*

	Music	History
1874	Verdi Requiem	
1875	Ravel born; Bizet *Carmen*; Bizet dies; Grieg *Peer Gynt* suites	
1876	Brahms Symphony No. 1; first performance at Bayreuth of Wagner's complete *Ring* cycle	Alexander Bell invents telephone
1877	Tchaikovsky *Swan Lake*; Saint-Saëns *Samson et Dalila*	Thomas Edison invents phonograph
1878	Brahms Violin Concerto; Wagner begins work on *Parsifal*	first use of electric street lighting
1879	Tchaikovsky *Eugene Onegin*	Austria-Hungary and Germany form Dual Alliance; Edison produces first electric light bulb
1880	Offenbach dies; Smetana *Má vlast*; Tchaikovsky *Romeo and Juliet* overture	Boer revolt against British in South Africa
1881	Mussorgsky dies; Offenbach *Les Contes d'Hoffmann* premiere	
1882	Stravinsky born; Wagner *Parsifal*	
1883	Wagner dies; Bruckner Symphony No. 7; Chabrier *España*	

Art and Architecture	Literature
ris Opéra completed (Charles Garnier); st Impressionist exhibition	Verlaine *Romances sans Paroles*; Hardy *Far from the Madding Crowd*
rot dies; Millet dies	
ert Memorial completed, London lbert Scott)	Mallarmé *L'Après-midi d'un faune*
urbet dies	
uschwanstein, Bavaria: imitation of a dieval castle for Ludwig II	
tural History Museum, London aterhouse)	Ibsen *A Doll's House*
	Flaubert dies; James *The Portrait of a Lady*
asso born; Manet *Bar at the Folies-gère*	Dostoevsky dies
net dies; Japanese exhibition in Paris	Stevenson *Treasure Island*

	Music	History
1884	Smetana dies; Massenet *Manon*	
1885		Benz and Daimler develop internal combustion engine
1886	Franck Violin Sonata	British Parliament rejects Irish Home Rule
1887	Verdi *Otello*; Fauré Requiem	
1888	Rimsky-Korsakov *Sheherazade*	Heinrich Hertz demonstrates existence of radio waves
1889	Strauss *Don Juan*	Universal Exhibition in Paris
1890	Mascagni *Cavalleria rusticana*	
1891		
1892	Tchaikovsky *The Nutcracker*; Leoncavallo *Pagliacci*	
1893	Tchaikovsky dies; Dvořák 'New World' Symphony; Sibelius *Karelia*	Henry Ford builds his first car; Keir Hardie founds Independent Labour Party in Britain; women granted vote in New Zealand
1894	Chabrier dies; Debussy *Prélude à l'après-midi d'un faune*	accession of Tsar Nicholas II in Russia; Dreyfus wrongly convicted of treason in France

Art and Architecture	Literature
	Victor Hugo dies; Zola *Germinal*
...hth and last Impressionist exhibition	Rimbaud *Illuminations*; Stevenson *Dr Jekyll and Mr Hyde*
	Strindberg *Miss Julie*
...n Gogh *Starry Night*; Eiffel Tower built	
...n Gogh dies	
	Rimbaud dies; Wilde *The Picture of Dorian Gray*
	Tennyson dies; G. and W. Grossmith *The Diary of a Nobody*
	Shaw *Arms and the Man*

	Music	History
1895		Lumière brothers invent cinematograph
1896	Bruckner dies; Puccini *La Bohème*	Henri Becquerel discovers radioactivity
1897	Brahms dies; Dukas *The Sorcerer's Apprentice*	
1898	Strauss *Ein Heldenleben*	Spanish-American War: Cuba gains independence, Puerto Rico and Philippines ceded to USA
1899	Sibelius Symphony No. 1, and premiere of *Finlandia*; Elgar 'Enigma' Variations	Boer War begins in South Africa
1900	Puccini *Tosca*; Debussy *Nocturnes*	build-up of German sea power begin
1901	Verdi dies; Ravel *Jeux d'eau*	Queen Victoria dies; Marconi makes first transatlantic radio transmissions
1902	Mahler Symphony No. 5; Debussy *Pelléas et Mélisande*	
1903		Wright Brothers make first successful flight in America; Emmeline Pankhurst founds Women's Social an Political Union
1904	Puccini *Madama Butterfly*; Mahler *Kindertotenlieder*	Emile Berliner replaces phonograph cylinders with discs

Art and Architecture	Literature
	Hardy *Jude the Obscure*
	Verlaine dies; Chekhov *The Seagull*
asgow School of Art begun (Charles ◦nnie Mackintosh)	Rostand *Cyrano de Bergerac*; Bram Stoker *Dracula*
	Mallarmé dies; James *The Turn of the Screw*
◦sley dies; Monet begins *Waterlilies* ◦ries at Giverny, paints views of the ◦ames	Nabokov born; Hemingway born
	Nietzsche dies
◦ulouse-Lautrec dies; beginning of ◦icasso's Blue Period	Strindberg *The Dance of Death*
	Zola dies
◦issarro dies; Gauguin dies	London *The Call of the Wild*; Shaw *Man and Superman*
	Chekhov *The Cherry Orchard*; Conrad *Nostromo*; Barrie *Peter Pan*

	Music	History
1905	Strauss *Salome*; Debussy *La Mer*	Bloody Sunday, St Petersburg: troops fire on workers
1906		Dreyfus retried, found not guilty of treason (France); first Russian parliament
1907	Grieg dies; Rachmaninov Symphony No. 2	Hague peace conference fails to secure arms limitation from Germany; Britain, France and Russia join in triple entente
1908	Rimsky-Korsakov dies; Elgar Symphony No. 1	Austria annexes Bosnia and Herzegovina
1909	Mahler Symphony No. 9; Rachmaninov Piano Concerto No. 3	Louis Blériot flies across English Channel
1910	Stravinsky *The Firebird*	
1911	Sibelius Symphony No. 4; Strauss *Der Rosenkavalier*; Stravinsky *Petrushka*	
1912	Massenet dies; Ravel *Daphnis and Chloe*	first Balkan War; *Titanic* sinks on maiden voyage
1913	Stravinsky *The Rite of Spring*	new state of Albania created
1914		Archduke Franz Ferdinand of Austria assassinated; World War I begins

Art and Architecture	Literature
atisse and others labelled 'Les Fauves' /ild beasts') in Paris	
zanne dies	
asso *Les Demoiselles d'Avignon*; ginning of Cubism	
	Forster *A Room with a View*
	Tolstoy dies; H.G. Wells *The History of Mr Polly*
ibition of Blaue Reiter group, Munich	
	Mann *Death in Venice*
	Proust *A la recherche du temps perdu* (part 1); Lawrence *Sons and Lovers*
	Joyce *A Portrait of the Artist as a Young Man*

Front Cover: Featured Music

Transcribed for legibility

These few bars, appearing right at the beginning of Wagner's *Tristan and Isolde* (website 12), represent a watershed in musical history.

In the second full bar of this extract, there is a chord containing the notes F, B, D sharp and G sharp. This one chord contains explosive implications for the development of music: for what exactly is the chord?

It is this question that has been debated ever since. Before this, chords could be labelled, so that their purpose within the confines of a particular key could be clearly understood. There were expectations of the way in which one chord would progress to another – so a 'dominant 7th' chord, based on the fifth note of the scale, would very likely lead to a 'tonic' chord, based on the first note of the scale, or 'keynote'. The ear could comprehend what was happening and would be comfortable with it. But this chord of Wagner's refuses to be labelled. It is ambiguous. What key are we

actually in? This was the first step in the rejection of 'tonality' (the whole idea of music being 'in a key') as a basis for musical composition, which would lead to further, radical developments in the twentieth century.

Wagner made the *sound* of harmony more important than its *function*.

The sound created at the beginning of this prelude is magical and distinctive. It introduces the beautiful yearning, sighing quality that is so representative of this work and appropriate for the unending but impossible love between Tristan and Isolde. The cellos enter with the first three notes, to be joined by the woodwind on the 'Tristan' chord. Though adapted in many ways, this chord appears throughout the whole opera, to be fully resolved only at the very end. The music, with its beautifully unsettled harmony, mirrors the state of the ill-fated lovers.

Composers of the Romantic Era

Albéniz, Isaac (1860–1909)
(*b.* Camprodón, Gerona, Spain; *d.* Cambo-les-Bains, France)

Balakirev, Mily (1837–1910)
(*b.* Nizhniy Novgorod, Russia; *d.* St Petersburg, Russia)

Beethoven, Ludwig van (1770–1827)
(*b.* Bonn, Germany; *d.* Vienna, Austria)

Bellini, Vincenzo (1801–1835)
(*b.* Catania, Italy; Puteaux, nr Paris, France)

Berlioz, Hector (1803–1869)
(*b.* Isère, France; *d.* Paris, France)

Bizet, Georges (1838–1875)
(*b.* Paris, France; *d.* Bougival, nr Paris, France)

Borodin, Alexander (1833–1887)
(*b.* St Petersburg, Russia; *d.* St Petersburg, Russia)

Brahms, Johannes (1833–1897)
(*b.* Hamburg, Germany; *d.* Vienna, Austria)

Bruckner, Anton (1824–1896)
(*b.* Ansfelden, nr Linz, Austria; *d.* Vienna, Austria)

Chopin, Fryderyk (1810–1849)
(*b.* Żelazowa Wola, nr Warsaw, Poland; *d.* Paris, France)

Cui, César (1835–1918)
(*b.* Vilnius, Lithuania; *d.* Petrograd [St Petersburg], Russia)

Debussy, Claude (1862–1918)
(*b.* St Germain-en-Laye, France; *d.* Paris, France)

Donizetti, Gaetano (1797–1848)
(*b.* Bergamo, Italy; *d.* Bergamo, Italy)

Dvořák, Antonín (1841–1904)
(*b.* Nelahozeves, nr Kralupy, Bohemia; *d.* Prague, Czech Republic)

Elgar, Sir Edward (1857–1934)
(*b.* Broadheath, nr Worcester, England; *d.* Worcester, England)

Falla, Manuel de (1876–1946)
(*b.* Cádiz, Spain; *d.* Alta Gracia, Argentina)

Fauré, Gabriel (1845–1924)
(*b.* Pamiers, Ariège, France; *d.* Paris, France)

Glinka, Mikhail Ivanovich (1804–1857)
(*b.* Novospasskoye, nr Yelnya, Smolensk district, Russia; *d.* Berlin, Germany)

Grieg, Edvard (1843–1907)
(*b.* Bergen, Norway; *d.* Bergen, Norway)

Liszt, Franz (1811–1886)
(*b.* Raiding, Hungary; *d.* Bayreuth, Germany)

Mahler, Gustav (1860–1911)
(*b.* Kalischt, nr Iglau [now Kaliště, Jihlava], Bohemia; *d.* Vienna, Austria)

Mendelssohn, Felix (1809–1847)
(*b.* Hamburg, Germany; *d.* Leipzig, Germany)

Mussorgsky, Modest (1839–1881)
(*b.* Karevo, Pskov district, Russia; *d.* St Petersburg, Russia)

Nielsen, Carl (1865–1931)
(*b.* Sortelung, nr Nørre Lyndelse, Funen, Denmark; *d.* Copenhagen, Denmark)

Parry, Sir Hubert (1848–1918)
(*b.* Bournemouth, England; *d.* Rustington, Sussex, England)

Puccini, Giacomo (1858–1924)
(*b.* Lucca, Italy; *d.* Brussels, Belgium)

Rachmaninov, Sergei (1873–1943)
(*b.* Oneg, Russia; *d.* Beverly Hills, CA, USA)

Ravel, Maurice (1875–1937)
(*b.* Ciboure, Basses-Pyrénées, France; *d.* Paris, France)

Rimsky-Korsakov, Nikolai (1844–1908)
(*b.* Tikhvin, Russia; *d.* Lyubensk, nr Luga [now Pskov district], Russia)

Rodrigo, Joaquín (1901–1999)
(*b.* Sagunto, Spain; *d.* Madrid, Spain)

Rossini, Gioachino (1792–1868)
(*b.* Pesaro, Italy; *d.* Passy, France)

Saint-Saëns, Camille (1835–1921)
(*b.* Paris, France; *d.* Algiers, Algeria)

Schoenberg, Arnold (1874–1951)
(*b.* Vienna, Austria; *d.* Los Angeles, USA)

Schubert, Franz (1797–1828)
(*b.* Vienna, Austria; *d.* Vienna, Austria)

Schumann, Clara [née Wieck] (1819–1896)
(*b.* Leipzig, Germany; *d.* Frankfurt, Germany)

Schumann, Robert (1810–1856)
(*b.* Zwickau, Saxony, Germany; *d.* Endenich, nr Bonn, Germany)

Sibelius, Jean (1865–1957)
(*b.* Hämeenlinna, Finland; *d.* Järvenpää, Finland)

Smetana, Bedřich (1824–1884)
(*b.* Litomyšl, Bohemia; *d.* Prague, Bohemia)

Stanford, Sir Charles Villiers (1852–1924)
(*b.* Dublin, Ireland; *d.* London, England)

Strauss, Richard (1864–1949)
(*b.* Munich, Germany; *d.* Garmisch-Partenkirchen, Germany)

Tchaikovsky, Pyotr Il'yich (1840–1893)
(*b.* Kamsko-Votkinsk, Vyatka province, Russia; *d.* St Petersburg, Russia)

Verdi, Giuseppe (1813–1901)
(*b.* Roncole, nr Busseto, Italy; *d.* Milan, Italy)

Wagner, Richard (1813–1883)
(*b.* Leipzig, Germany; *d.* Venice, Italy)

Weber, Carl Maria von (1786–1826)
(*b.* Eutin, Germany; *d.* London, England)

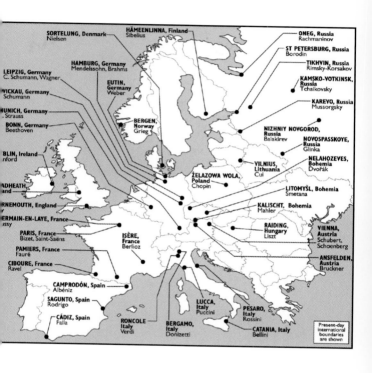

Map showing birthplaces of Romantic composers

Glossary

Adagio	slow
Allegro	fast but not excessively
Alto	the second-highest voice in a four-part choir
Andante	slowish, at a moderate walking pace
Aria	solo song, generally as part of an opera or oratorio
Bar (USA: measure)	the visual division of metre into successive units, marked off on a page of music by vertical lines; thus in triple metre (the grouping of music into groups of three, as in 3/4, 3/8 etc.) the three main beats will always be accommodated in the space between two vertical lines.
Baritone	a singer whose range lies between that of a tenor and bass
Baroque period	the era of western classical music, roughly from 1600 to 1750
Bass	the lowest form of male voice, the term is also used to describe the lowest part (or less specifically the lowest register) in any chord or piece.
Beat	the unit of pulse (the underlying 'throb' of music)
Bel canto	literally 'beautiful singing', referring to the Italian vocal style in the eighteenth and nineteenth centuries that emphasised fine phrasing, technique and beauty of tone
Cadence	a coming to rest on a particular note or key, as in the standard 'Amen' at the end of a hymn

Cadenza a relatively brief, often virtuosic solo passage in a concerto or operatic aria

Canon a piece of music in which a melody is played and then imitated by one or more instruments after a set time

Cantata a work in several movements for accompanied voice or voices (from the Latin/Italian *musica cantata*, 'sung music')

Chamber music music for small groups of players, like a string quartet or a piano trio; so called because it was originally played in the 'chamber' or home

Character pieces a term loosely applied to relatively short, mostly piano, pieces typical of nineteenth-century Romanticism (but also popular throughout much of the twentieth century) in which mood may be said to predominate over form – though many such pieces adhere to a straightforward ternary (A–B–A) structure

Chorale a hymn-like choral piece

Chord basically any simultaneous combination of three or more notes; chords are analogous to words, just as the notes of which they consist are analogous to letters.

Chromatic (chromaticism) notes (and the using of notes) which are not contained in the standard 'diatonic' scales forming the basis of most western music; for example, in the scale of C major (which uses only the white keys of a piano) every black key on a piano is 'chromatic'.

Classical era loosely, the period of western classical music between the death of J.S. Bach in 1750 and that of Beethoven in 1827 (overlapping with the Romantic era) in which the complex polyphony of the Baroque era gave way to the simpler textures of melody-and-accompaniment, and symmetry of form and proportion became a primary concern. The era was dominated by the concept of sonata form and is primarily distinguished from the succeeding Romantic era by its relative objectivity of approach.

Concerto a work for solo instrument and orchestra, generally in three movements (fast–slow–fast)

Contralto	a female alto
Counterpoint (contrapuntal)	the interweaving of separate horizontal melodic lines, as opposed to the accompaniment of a top-line (horizontal) melody by a series of (vertical) chords
Crescendo	getting louder
Development	the middle section in sonata form, normally characterised by progression through several keys
Diatonic	using only the scale steps of the prevailing 'key notes' of the regular scale
Dynamics	the gradations of softness and loudness, and the terms that indicate them
Étude	the French equivalent of 'study', widely adopted for pieces whose primary aim is the development of a particular technical aspect
Exposition	the first section in sonata form, where the main themes are introduced
Expressionism	a term applied to trends in all art forms around World War I, in which turbulence and chaos are prominent
Fantasy, Fantasie, Fantasia	a free form, often of an improvisatory nature, following the composer's fancy rather than any preordained structures. There are some later fantasies, however, like Schubert's 'Wanderer' Fantasy and Schumann's Fantasie in C, both for the piano, that are tightly integrated works incorporating fully fledged sonata forms, scherzos, fugues etc.
Finale	a generic term for last movement
Flat	the sign showing that a note must be lowered by a semitone from its 'natural' position, i.e., the nearest lower neighbour of most notes in a diatonic scale
Form	the overall shape or structure of a piece
Forte; Fortissimo	loud; very loud
Fugue (fugal)	an imitative work in several overlapping parts. Fugue derives from the same principle as the common

'round' or canon, though it can be much more complicated. It begins with a solo tune or short theme (known as the 'subject'). When this has been played, the second 'voice' (singer or instrument) answers with the same theme (subject), but in a different key. While this second voice is playing or singing the subject, the first continues with a new tune (known as a 'countersubject'). In the overlapping scheme of things, this is equivalent to the second phrase of a round or canon ('Dormez-vous' in *Frère Jacques*; 'See how they run' in *Three Blind Mice*). When subject and countersubject complete their counterpoint, a third 'voice' enters with its own statement of the subject. Voice two now repeats voice one's countersubject, while voice one introduces a new countersubject. And so it goes, alternating with 'episodes' in which the various voices combine in free counterpoint, but with no full statements of the subject in any voice.

Furiant an exuberant Bohemian folk dance with alternating duple and triple metre. The Czech name has no connection with the English word 'furious', nor has the character of the dance.

Grand opéra (grand opera) a form of grandiose and spectacular opera, generally dealing with famous historical events, movements, heroes, or biblical/legendary figures and featuring lavish scenery, costumes, stage machinery etc. A forerunner of the great Hollywood epics of Cecil B. de Mille, it is mainly associated with the Paris Opéra of the mid-nineteenth century, where its principal exemplars were Rossini, Donizetti, Gounod, Meyerbeer, Massenet and Verdi. The term is also applied to such similar but non-French operas as Wagner's *Rienzi*.

Harmony (harmonic) the simultaneous sounding of notes to make a chord; harmonies (chords) often serve as expressive or atmospheric 'adjectives', describing or giving added meaning to the notes of a melody, which, in turn, may be likened to nouns and verbs.

Homophony (homophonic) when all parts move at once, giving the effect of a melody (the successive top notes) accompanied by chords

Idée fixe a recurring theme

Impressionism a term borrowed from French painting to describe the fluid, progressive music being written by composers such as Debussy at the end of the nineteenth century

Impromptu an arbitrary term for a substantial piano piece in ternary (A–B–A) form

Incidental music in the theatre, music to be performed as part of a spoken drama

Intermezzo originally an instrumental interlude in an opera, the term also applies, fairly loosely, to self-contained piano pieces, generally following a ternary (A–B–A) pattern. Brahms gave the name to many of his short piano pieces.

Interval the distance in pitch between notes; for example, the interval between C and G is a 5th (C[1], D[2], E[3], F[4], G[5]).

Key pieces of western classical music are usually in particular keys, based on the notes of the western scale (C major, G minor etc.); a key is a piece's home – the music can travel away from it, but usually comes back in the end (also see 'tonality').

Leitmotif a theme used recurrently to identify and amplify a character, situation or object, usually in operas – especially those of Wagner.

Libretto the literary text of an opera or oratorio

Lied/Lieder a form of German art song, extremely popular in the nineteenth century, in which a poetical text is generally reflected in or actually illustrated by the piano accompaniment, which may be of considerable complexity, prominence and even virtuosity (Schubert's setting of Goethe's *Erlkönig* being perhaps the most famous example). The intimate connection between words and music, enhanced by the sophistication of the latter, is a definitive characteristic. In true Lieder (the plural of Lied), the so-called accompaniment is as important as the song – in Schubert's case, sometimes even more important. Other great Lieder composers were Schumann, Brahms and Hugo Wolf.

Major see 'modes'

March a piece in duple metre, originally, as the name suggests, composed to accompany and regulate military marching

Mazurka a Polish folk dance in triple metre, in which the accent is shifted to the weak beats of the bar

Measure see 'bar'

Melody (melodic) a tune (tuneful)

Metre (metrical) the grouping together of beats in recurrent units of two, three, four, six, etc.; metre is the pulse of music

Mezzo-soprano a singer whose range lies between that of soprano and alto

Minor see 'modes'

Minuet, menuet an originally French dance, in the folk tradition, it can be seen as an ancestor of the waltz: both have three beats in a bar, and an elegance from being played and developed for years in royal courts of Europe.

Modes the names given to the particular arrangement of notes within a scale. Every key in western classical music has two versions, the major and the minor mode; the decisive factor is the size of the interval between the key note (the tonic, the foundation on which scales are built) and the third degree of the scale: if it is compounded of two whole tones (as in C–E [C–D/D–E]) the mode is major; if the third tone is made up of one-and-a-half tones (C–E flat) the mode is minor; in general, the minor mode is darker, more 'serious', more moody, more obviously dramatic than the major. The church modes prevalent in the Middle Ages comprise various combinations of major and minor and are less obviously dynamic; these appear only rarely in music after the Baroque period (1600–1750) and have normally been used by composers to create some kind of archaic effect.

Modulation the movement from one key to another, generally involving at least one pivotal chord common to both keys

Motif, motive a kind of musical acorn; a melodic/rhythmic figure too brief to constitute a proper theme, but one on which themes are built; a perfect example is the beginning of Beethoven's Symphony No. 5: ta-ta-ta *dah*; ta-ta-ta *dah*.

Movement a primary, self-contained division of a larger work, comparable to a chapter in a book

New German School a group of progressive musicians in the mid-nineteenth century – Liszt effectively headed the movement, along with Wagner and Berlioz. The group stood in opposition to more conservative composers such as Brahms.

Nocturne a piece suggesting night, usually quiet and reflective; Field first used the term for his pieces, which were important forerunners of Chopin's.

Opera basically, a sung play – a stage work that combines words, drama, music (with singers and orchestra), and often elaborate scenery

Oratorio an extended choral/orchestral setting of religious texts in a dramatic and semi-operatic fashion; the most famous example is Handel's *Messiah*.

Orchestration the art of using instruments in the orchestra for specific expressive, dramatic, colouristic, structural and textural purposes; the arrangement for orchestra of works originally written for other media, e.g. keyboard, choir etc.

Overture a single orchestral movement, normally designed to introduce an opera, oratorio or a play with music, and often based on themes to follow. The term applies also to a free-standing concert work, generally alluding in its title to a literary, pictorial or emotional theme, as in Mendelssohn's *The Hebrides*.

Phrase	a smallish group of notes (generally accommodated by the exhalation of a single breath) that form a unit of melody, as in 'Twinkle, twinkle, little star' (phrase 1) 'How I wonder what you are' (phrase 2)
Phrasing	shaping a piece of music into phrases
Piano; pianissimo	soft; very soft
Piano quintet	a piece for piano and four other instruments, usually a string quartet (two violins, viola and cello)
Piano trio	generally a trio comprising piano, violin and cello, though different instrumental combinations do occur
Pizzicato	string plucked with the finger rather than bowed
Polka	an originally Bohemian duple-metre dance for couples. It has no connection with Poland, as many seem to think, and was made world-famous by the Viennese Strauss family.
Polonaise	originally a Polish dance, of a stately, processional character. It was developed outside Poland in the nineteenth century, and Chopin wrote many.
Polyphony	music with interweaving parts
Prelude	literally, a piece that is heard first and introduces another piece (as in the standard 'Prelude and Fugue'); however, the name has been applied (most famously by Bach and Chopin) to describe free-standing short pieces.
Presto; prestissimo	very fast; even faster
programme music	music specifically designed to illustrate a story, poem – that is, music or other narrative dependent on extra-musical sources (see also 'symphonic poem')
Recapitulation	the third section in sonata form, where the main themes come home (see 'sonata form')
Recitative	a short narrative section in an opera or oratorio normally sung by a solo voice and preceding an aria; the rhythm is in a free style, being dictated by the words.

Requiem the Roman Catholic Mass for the dead. Many composers, including Berlioz, Brahms, Dvořák, Fauré and Britten, have written requiems for concert and ceremonial use.

Reminiscence motif a tune assigned to a particular character and heard whenever that character appeared on stage (precursor to the more sophisticated leitmotif)

Rhapsody an often loosely constructed, sectional and self-contained piece of a romantic, narrative character

Rhythm (rhythmic) that aspect of music concerned with duration and accent; notes may be of many contrasting lengths and derive much of their character and definition from patterns of accentuation and emphasis determined by the composer.

Romance a term loosely applied to many types of self-contained instrumental works of a generally intimate and tender character

Romantic era loosely, the period from later Beethoven to the outbreak of World War I. Unlike the more 'objective' Classical era preceding it, Romanticism, as its name suggests, placed a premium on emotional content, prizing spontaneity oef feeling and vividness of expression over the academic disciplines of preordained forms. The taste was for confectionery miniatures and lavish dramas, sensuality of sound and monumental forces, illustrative 'symphonic poems' and extravagant feats of virtuosity.

Scale from the Italian word *scala* ('ladder'); a series of adjacent notes (A–B–C–D–E–F etc.) moving up or down; these 'ladders' provide the basic cast of characters from which melodies are made and keys established.

Scherzo a fast dance-movement in triple metre, like the minuet and the waltz, in which the definitive unit of measurement is the bar rather than the beats within it. After Beethoven, it usurped the place of the minuet in the Classical symphony and sonata. Schubert, Chopin and Brahms, among others, also wrote self-contained scherzos for the piano.

Schubertiads   concerts organised by Schubert's friends in which his chamber music was played

Semitone   half a tone; the smallest interval commonly used in western classical music

Serenade   originally a nocturnal song sung by a suitor beneath the window of his beloved, it came in the eighteenth century to denote a multi-movement orchestral work freer in construction than a symphony and generally light and agreeable in character, often designed for performance outdoors on summer evenings. The best known is probably Mozart's *Eine kleine Nachtmusik*. Brahms, Tchaikovsky, Dvořák, Elgar and many others wrote serenades of similar character in the nineteenth century.

Sharp   the sign showing that a note must be raised by a semitone from its 'natural' position, i.e. the nearest upper neighbour of most notes in a diatonic scale

Sonata   generally, a three- or four-movement instrumental work for one or two instruments, in which one movement (from the last quarter of the eighteenth century onwards) is in sonata form

Sonata form   also known as 'sonata-allegro' and 'first movement' form, this was the dominant form throughout the second half of the eighteenth century and the first third of the nineteenth. It is basically a ternary (three-part) design in which the last part is a modified repeat of the first. The three sections of the standard sonata form are called Exposition, Development and Recapitulation. The Exposition, which may be prefaced by a slow introduction, is based on the complementary tensions of two opposing keys. Each key-group generally has its own themes, but this contrast is of secondary importance. In movements in the major mode, the secondary key is almost invariably the dominant. When the key of the movement is in the minor mode, the secondary key will almost always be the relative major. The Exposition always ends in the secondary key, never on the tonic. In most sonata-form movements, the main themes of the two key-groups will also be of a contrasting character. If the first main theme is blustery or military, the second, in the complementary key, is likely to be more serene and contemplative. The Development is altogether more free and unpredictable. In most cases, true to its name, it takes themes or ideas from the Exposition and 'develops' them, but it may ignore the themes of the Exposition altogether. What it will have is a notably increased sense of harmonic instability, drifting, or in some cases struggling, through a number of different keys before delivering us back to the tonic for the Recapitulation. Since the Recapitulation lacks the tonal tensions of the Exposition, the themes themselves, now all in the same key, take on a new relationship. In its prescribed resolution of family (tonal) conflicts, sonata form may be seen as the most Utopian of all musical structures.

Song cycle   a sequence of accompanied songs connected by a common subject, often of a cumulatively narrative nature, the poems generally being by a single poet

Soprano   generally, the highest type of female voice

String quartet   a piece composed for two violins, viola and cello, in which one movement, usually the first, is in sonata form

String quintet   generally a piece for string quartet plus an additional viola, but some (notably Schubert's in C major) use an additional cello instead. As with the string quartet, the first movement is usually in sonata form.

Sturm und Drang   literally 'storm and stress'. The term denotes a literary and musical movement in the eighteenth century cultivating the expression of turbulent, intense and dramatic emotions, and has come to be more loosely applied to any work of art of a comparable character.

Suite   an instrumental piece comprising several movements while not conforming to a fixed large-scale pattern as in the symphony or sonata. In the eighteenth century the term denoted specifically a sequence of dance movements but is now used to describe any fairly loose assemblage of movements, often from an opera, ballet, play or film.

Symphony a sonata for orchestra, generally in four movements (see also 'sonata form')

Symphonic poem, tone poem an orchestral form in which a poem or programme provides a narrative or illustrative basis

Technique physical skill in playing an instrument

Tempo the speed of music

Tenor the higher of the two standard male voices, the lower being the bass

Ternary form a three-section structure (A–B–A) in which the final part is an exact or nearly exact repetition of the first

Texture generally used to describe the prevailing pattern of notes, as in a 'polyphonic' texture (the interweaving of melodic strands, as in a round, canon or fugue) or the more densely packed 'chordal' style of the standard church hymn. The term is also used to describe the density of notes. Thus many 'chordal' notes sounding together and closely spaced in pitch are often described as creating a 'thick' texture, whereas a combination of fewer and more widely spaced notes may be described as being 'light'.

Theme a melody used as a basis for various kinds of variation and development or to fulfil a particular structural function, as in a 'transitional' theme used to connect two tunes in different keys

Time see 'metre'

Time signature the symbol (always a fraction) at the beginning of a piece, bar or phrase which indicates the metrical grouping of beats (what 'time' the music is in). Thus 4/4 designates a pulse of four crotchets (quarter notes), 3/8 a pulse of three quavers (eighth notes) , and so on.

Tonality put at its broadest, tonality has to do with a kind of tonal solar system in which each note (or 'planet'), each rung of the scale, has a relationship with one particular note (or 'sun'), which is known as the 'keynote' or 'tonic'. This is the music's home – it begins here, and comes back here at the end. When this planetary system is based on the note C, the key-note, or tonic, is C and the music is said to be 'in the key of C'. The composer can move to other keys (modulation) which sometimes creates a feeling of unrest – this is resolved when the music comes back to the key in which it started.

Tone colour, timbre   that property of sound which distinguishes a horn from a piano, a violin from a xylophone, etc.

Tone, whole tone   a major 2nd interval – the sum of two semitones, as in the first two notes of *Frère Jacques*

Transcription   a musical work copied out in notation usually with some change to the layout (e.g. a piano transcription of an orchestral work, in which the piano part absorbs all those originally for orchestra); Liszt made many transcriptions.

Variation   any decorative or otherwise purposeful alteration of a note, rhythm, timbre etc.

Variation forms   there are four basic types of variation:
1) those in which the original tune is clothed in a sequence of stylistic and textural dresses (ornamental turns, decorative scale passages, rhythmic, textural and tempo alterations, and so on) while the chief outline of the melody, the original harmonies, and the overall form of the theme are preserved, though the mode (major or minor) may sometimes be altered. The same techniques of variation can be applied, within the given limits, even to those elements that are retained from the original theme. The bass line, for instance, may be amplified by a trill, fast or slow, or be doubled in octaves, and the basic chords of the original harmonies may be seasoned with decorative notes adjacent to those of the original. This form is known generally as melodic variation. Almost all variation sets of the Classical period are of this kind, Mozart's being perhaps the best known.
2) those in which the harmonic pattern of the theme is preserved while the melody, tempo, rhythm, texture

(chords or intertwining melodic lines) and mode
(major/minor) may change beyond recognition
3) those in which the theme is not a self-sufficient
melody but either a constantly reiterated bass line
(above which the upper parts may change) or a series
of chords (whose harmonic sequence and unvarying
rhythm is reiterated, unchanged, throughout the
composition). This form of variation is called either
passacaglia or chaconne (in the Baroque era the two
terms were used interchangeably).
4) those in which only a part of the original theme (a
single melodic phrase, a motto rhythm, a structural
form) is retained as a basis for variation, all other
aspects and parts being subject to considerable
transformation

Virtuoso   a musician of exceptional technical skill

Waltz   originally a popular ballroom dance in triple metre, it
also exists in the form of 'concert' waltzes, such as
those by Chopin and Brahms, which were never
intended for actual dancing.

About the Author

David McCleery studied music at Manchester University before embarking on a career in arts administration. After various jobs with orchestras, artists' agencies and festivals, he joined Chester Music and Novello music publishers where he developed a keen interest in working with composers, including John Tavener, Richard Rodney Bennett and Thea Musgrave. That interest continues today, although he has moved to the field of media music and works for a management company for film and television composers. When time permits, he undertakes freelance writing projects. For Naxos, he has written *A Portrait of John Tavener*, as well as the Romantic and Twentieth-Century editions of the 'Discover' series.

Index

Also Available

Discover Early Music

by Lucien Jenkins

www.naxosbooks.com

Also Available

Beethoven: His Life and Music
by Jeremy Siepmann

Book + 2 CDs + website

for more details or to buy, visit
www.naxosbooks.com

Also Available

Chopin: His Life and Music

by Jeremy Nicholas

Book + 2 CDs + website

for more details or to buy, visit

www.naxosbooks.com

Also Available

Wagner: His Life and Music

by Stephen Johnson

Book + 2 CDs + website

for more details or to buy, visit

www.naxosbooks.com

Also Available

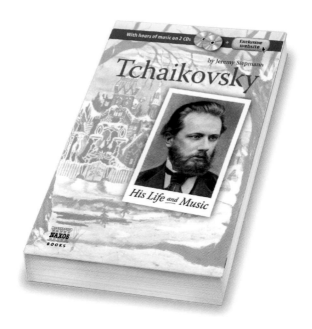

Tchaikovsky: His Life and Music

by Jeremy Siepmann

Book + 2 CDs + website

for more details or to buy, visit

www.naxosbooks.com